SECOND

EDITION

Desktop

DESIGN

GETTING

THE

PROFESSIONAL

LOOK

Brian Cookman

BLUEPRINT

An Imprint of Chapman & Hall

Published by Blueprint, an imprint of
Chapman & Hall, 2-6 Boundary Row, London SE1 8HN

Chapman & Hall, 2-6 Boundary Row, London SE1 8HN, UK

Blackie Academic & Professional, Wester Cleddens Road,
Bishopbriggs, Glasgow G64 2NZ, UK

Chapman & Hall Inc., 29 West 35th Street, New York NY10001, USA

Chapman & Hall Japan, Thomson Publishing Japan, Hirakawacho Nemoto
Building, 6F, 1-7-11 Hirakawa-cho, Chiyoda-ku, Tokyo 102, Japan

Chapman & Hall Australia, Thomas Nelson Australia, 102 Dodds Street,
South Melbourne, Victoria 3205, Australia

Chapman & Hall India, R. Seshadri, 32 Second Main Road, CIT East,
Madras 600 035, India

First edition 1990
Reprinted 1991
Second edition 1993

© 1990, 1993 Brian Cookman

Printed in Great Britain at the University Press, Cambridge

ISBN 0 948905 84 0

A catalogue record for this book is available from the British Library

Library of Congress Cataloging-in-Publication data available

Contents

INTRODUCTION   2

Chapter One
DESIGN BASICS
- Shapes in typography   6
- Grids   9
- Templates   12
- File management   13
- Hyphenation and justification   14
- Type   17
- Kerning   20
- Typesize   21
- Crossheads   22
- Typefaces   24
- Matching the face to the job   25
- Emphasis   28
- Images   34
- Scanning   38
- Colour scanning   39
- Optical character recognition   39
- Drawing packages   40
- Graphs and charts   42
- Cropping   43
- Rules, boxes and tints   44
- Colour   48
- Reversals   56

Chapter Two
DTP IN ACTION
- House style   60
- Logos   60
- Letterheads   64
- Forms, invoices and questionnaires   67
- Pamphlets, flyers and tickets   70
- Catalogues and price lists   73
- Advertisements   74
- Newspapers and magazines   80
- Templates   82
- Sales brochures   90
- Company reports   94
- Manuals and small books   99
- Presentations, slides and graphs   103

Chapter Three
BEYOND THE SCREEN
- Bureaux   107
- Laser printers and typesetters   109
- Disk conversion   111
- Modems   112
- Presentation and binding   114
- Health and safety   116
- The future and electronic publishing   118

GLOSSARY   120

INDEX   124

CREDITS   126

Introduction

Whenever I'm asked for advice on desktop publishing my first response is the analogy of giving someone a superb target rifle and assuming they will immediately be a brilliant marksman. It doesn't work like that. Technology has equipped us with wonderful hardware and software — enough for any design brief — and yet many people purchase a system and think it will take over their agency's work in days. Or worse still, they give the job to someone from the typing pool and expect them to be an award winner in weeks. Unfortunately, design sense, although often innate, has to be learned and even if already understood, must be applied to this new discipline.

Desktop publishing could really be defined as 'Computerised Integration of Text and Graphics' or 'Integrated Publishing Systems'. This sounds simple enough but I remember in the early 1980s, going to one of the first college courses on this subject. I was a designer for a leading group of computer magazines and had the usual arty loathing of machines and their usurping the traditional methods of casting-off, cut and paste, hand-and-eye and taste. The computer we needed to draw and manipulate simple images took up a large room and I had to learn basic FORTRAN and algorithms to manipulate drawings. Integrating text with graphics, however, was virtually impossible. Now, some ten years later, a PC computer with a tiny footprint can do any task required of it — almost instantly. I tried the earliest systems…and I was hooked.

Most designers have a dislike of computers, they think they are inhuman and unnatural. If, however, they are taught to use DTP as a form of design tool, they will find they have a super rubdown lettering system, with wrap-around type, easy drawing ability and simple, accurate rules, tints and boxes — all immediately available at the touch of a key or the move of a mouse. No hand can draw as accurate a box, as sharp a rule or lay a tint as simply.

The DTP system replaces smelly adhesives, ever-blunting scalpels and the eternally shaking drawing pen — and I, for one, say good riddance. Two years ago, I predicted that any designer not using a DTP system by 1992 was in danger of extinction, and I think events have proved me right. The old methods have become almost as anachronistic as loose type. I also consider DTP as revolutionary as Caxton's first printing press. He took the power of literacy from the Church and gave it to the common man. DTP has done the same. Now an individual can produce high quality publishing cheaply and effectively to combat the power of the big boys. The media now belongs to everybody.

That said, however, there are limitations. The old tools will never go completely. At the time of writing, it is still simpler and of higher quality to have the repro house strip in images than use the DTP scanned type. Also, laser prints won't replace a bromide or film for sharpness but these problems we'll meet and overcome in this book.

I intend to show the best way to use a desktop system with regard to design. A lot of the wheezes I describe are hard-won tricks I've developed over the years and hopefully, will save you many frustrating hours. The book is not intended to be for any particular system, most of those available will handle the designs without any trouble, any special feature used is mentioned.

Remember, Cookman's First Law of DTP Design: 'It is not the computer's fault - it's yours!'

Cookman's Second Law is: 'If it works — use it. If it doesn't — scrap it.'

A final caveat. DTP is addictive. Once you get the hang of handling it all, you will find you've missed your lunch or last train because you were enjoying yourself.

Brian Cookman, 1992

Design Basics

Good design is *EFFECTIVE COMMUNICATION*.

You should remember this and meditate upon it. Let this fact soak into your soul. It must be your constant companion.

Design is the way we communicate, usually the written word, to the reader in such a way as to encourage their interest and desire to read. It can't be more basic than that. We must convey a message as simply and attractively as possible on the printed page, giving information and enjoyment. We make shapes of type and symbols of images so that the overall 'picture' is attractive and desirable. Then it involves the reader with the author. Design is the interpreter, the go-between.

But design must be at the same time invisible! Yes, I know it's confusing, but what this means is that it shouldn't be obvious or obtrusive. If you gawk at the layout of a page, strictly speaking, the design isn't working.

So whether we are working on a letterhead or a company report, if the design makes it illegible or boring, then the reader will give up and we have failed.

Also, try lots of variations of the design. The wonder of DTP is that the time saved in production can be used on experimentation. Print one example and move on. But you must follow DTP's Third Law — 'Save, save, save.'

Finally, remember - *EFFECTIVE COMMUNICATION*.

Here are the basic elements of a page, the lines represent type...

...which can be made into mock columns.

Pictures can be indicated by a tint box and headlines by a black rule.

So, we start with a page of text.

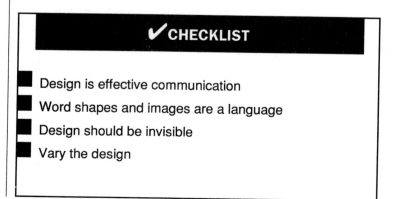

✔ CHECKLIST

- Design is effective communication
- Word shapes and images are a language
- Design should be invisible
- Vary the design

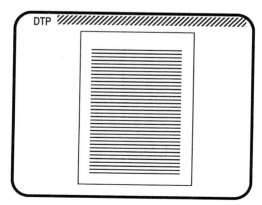

4

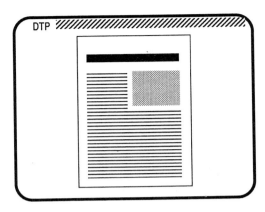

Left, lay out is the conventional head, text, picture ranged right. Dull.

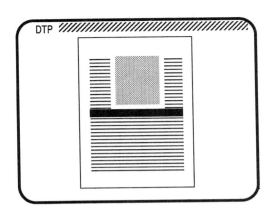

This time, on the right, the picture takes precedence, but the headline gets lost along the bottom. Clumsy.

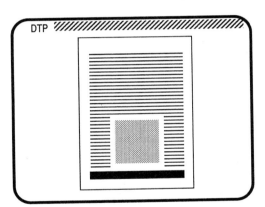

Left puts the headline on the bottom of the page. Downright ugly.

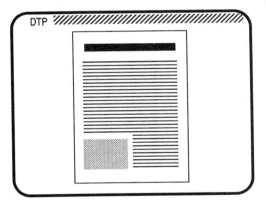

Here we try to range the picture along the bottom and left. This looks terrible because the picture seems to be falling out of the page.

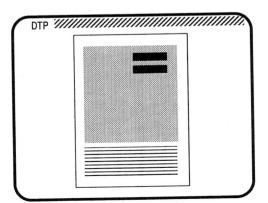

This time the picture takes precedence, you can blow up a picture and make it the background to the text. Mind type sizes if you do this.

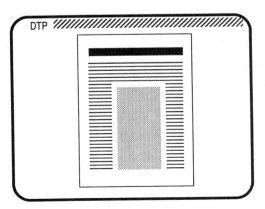

Right, has the picture re-cropped and centred, yet it does not 'fall out'.

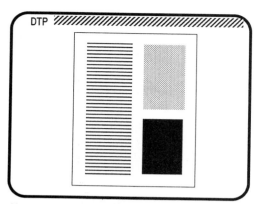

Here we have a three element layout. Black shows the headline block, tint for the picture and lines for the text

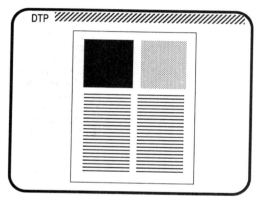

This is more informal. The header draws you down to the text then up to the next column and finally to the picture.

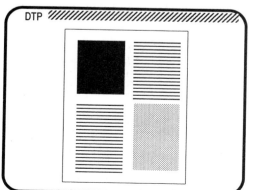

SHAPES IN TYPOGRAPHY

A fundamental concept of typography is that we are working with blocks or shapes. A block of text can be as dark or light as you wish, long or short, fat or thin but it is fundamentally a 'block'. Think of them as the building bricks we used to play with as children. Designers will be familiar with this concept but it is worth noting that with DTP the speed and accuracy of type block placing makes layouts fast and simple to re-make. Instead of having to send off copy to the typesetters for new galleys in a different width/size/style, you can do it immediately on screen.

Try calling up a blank page and draw grey boxes within the shape. Observe how, by repositioning them, or shortening them, they change the 'feel' of the page. Now try adding a black box or two and maybe a heavy black rule to look like a headline. Now try including open boxes for pictures Move them around, see how easy it is? Old hands shouldn't be wary of this freedom but dive in — let your imagination run riot. You can change everything at the touch of a button or mouse.

You should also consider whether your design is a spread (two pages side-by-side) or a single page and if it is left or right bound. This could effect your design.

What we should remember is that the reader must not become lost. The eye should follow a simple route, not a maze. If it is too tricky the eye will say 'Skip it.' At the same time avoid being dull. If everything is the same shape or size the eye will find it difficult to decide which way to go, so make the design an easy path to follow, with signposts, stiles and occasional benches for resting. These are guidelines but there are no hard and fast rules, make them as you go. Feel free to experiment and be daring!

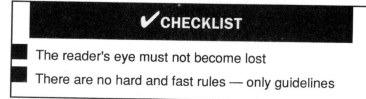

✔ CHECKLIST

The reader's eye must not become lost

There are no hard and fast rules — only guidelines

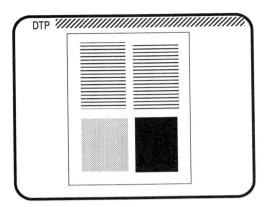

This is not recommended as the text is not strong enough to carry the design. The picture is lost in the corner and the headline comes too late.

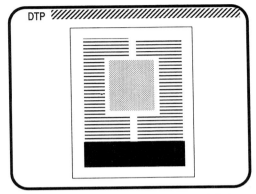

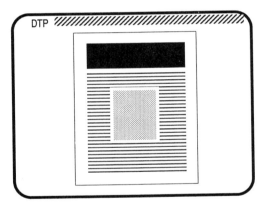

Here we try the head as a two line top with the picture floating in the middle of the page. Although I've tried it with full width setting rather than two columns, this is my favourite.

Same as left, but reversing the headline's position. Not bad - but the heading type face would have to be a 'grabber' or it would get lost.

Nobody said that you couldn't re-size the heading and picture. Remember rules are made to broken. This one could work very well.

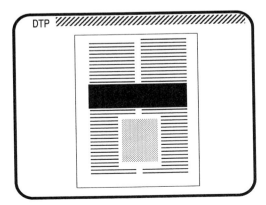

More unusual variant of the above. Headline runs across the middle and the picture floats lower down. A trifle bottom heavy.

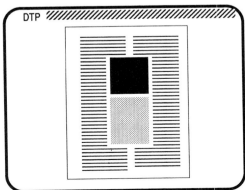

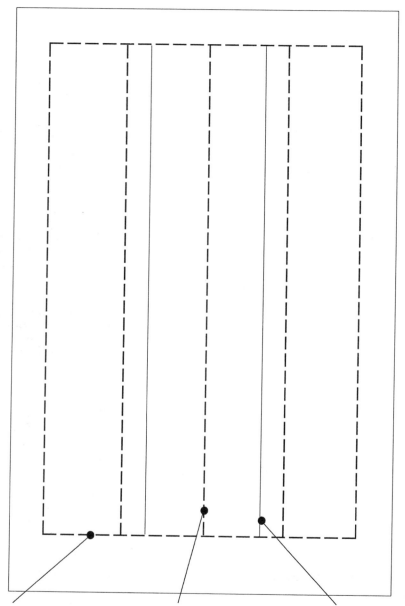

There is an optical illusion where, if the top and bottom margins are equal it looks top heavy, so allow slightly more on the bottom margin.

Finally, don't forget to increase the inside edge if the page is to be bound in any way, to allow for the gutter.

Begin drawing up a grid with your margins. Keep in mind you can be limited by the printing area of your laser printer.

The dotted lines represent the underlying four column grid. Can be used as two columns or three.

Main grid is in three columns, again can be used as two plus one as well as three together.

GRIDS

All designs require one more important factor, an anchor. This stops the design floating away into infinity. The usual 'anchor' is the grid, holding the style and consistency of the page or pages together.

Depending on the brief, type can be run in columns, giving a different style to the page. Type width also affects the readability of text, and is best between 36 - 50 characters per line (cpl). It is difficult to read a line over 75 cpl width so most magazines usually run around 40 per column regardless of the style or measure. The guideline is thin columns for small type, and wider for large type.

This is where the grid comes in — right at the beginning. In any publication we must have consistency, otherwise the layout becomes confusing to the reader. Margins should be the same, typefaces shouldn't change unless there is a good reason.

A grid is an invisible framework, a set of parameters which the type on the page follows rigidly. Grids aren't actually invisible, it's just that they don't print in the final run-out. But they give the pages consistency, a sense of organisation. However, strictly adhering to the grid doesn't mean you have no freedom.

Your grid can be as complex as you wish, allowing all sorts of measures and variations. This is how a publication can have different elements, and stories and yet retain an overall style or look, issue to issue.

All this applies equally to advertisements or any piece of design, not just journals. It is a worthwhile exercise to create a grid for every new job you start. Most make-up software carries some standard grids and layouts to get you started. Use them until you feel confident enough to strike out on your own.

The reason we use grids is to make it easier for the eye to scan a line. Too long a line and it soon gets tired. Here we see the tonal shapes of two and three column grids

✔ KEYPOINTS

Grids act as a page's anchor

Grids ensure consistency, even complex grids can be flexible, and invisible

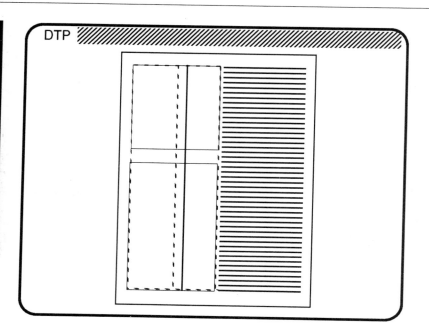

You can see the grid showing through a basic layout, using the four column grid and halving it. In this case making room for a couple of pictures or graphics.

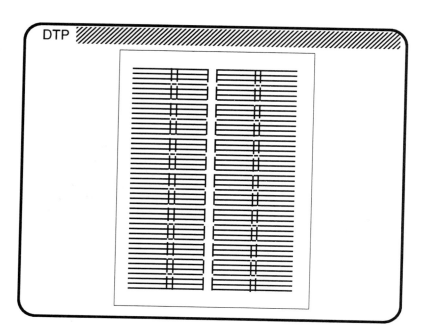

Here, the four column grid is used in a wide two column layout. Unbelievably dull and very common but, I suppose, useful in reports as at least it breaks up the page — just!

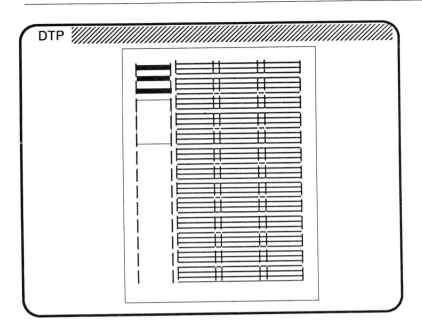

Here I've used the four column grid as one by three for the text and the remainder for headline and picture. This is a good alternative when you have not much in the way of graphics to give the page a lift. Don't be afraid to use the white space creatively

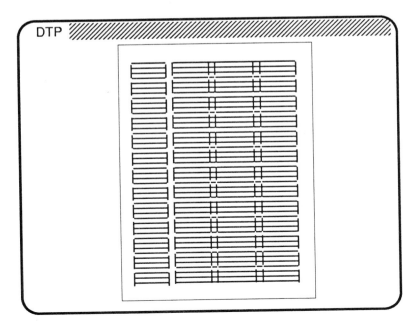

Finally, I've tried it with a thin column of text - good for boxed copy or intros. This is best when you have no graphics or lots of notes or sub-text, especially boxed in a thin tint box. Try a type change such as bold or italicised faces in the thin column

TEMPLATES

The whole point of a grid is to act as a cornerstone of the 'template' which is the basis of all jobs. Try to think of it as a jelly mould. We should spend a lot of effort getting the mould just right and then, every time the job comes along, we can pour in thin jelly and leave the mould to do the rest. Don't re-invent the wheel each time the job is needed. (By 'thin jelly' I mean copy that has been subbed and checked for spelling, with no indents, no double paragraphs and so on. These settings are applied far more accurately at the template stage.)

The template, or mould, ensures consistency of layout and type. There is nothing more amateur than a publication that changes from page to page, giving the ransom-note look. There is a system I have devised that is well worth following. The problem for most desktop designers is that they keep having to go backwards and forwards in the document, changing things they have forgotten or doing things they should have done in the first place. By following this method you will work in the correct order and find layouts much easier.

Finally, preparation is everything. The more effort you put into the template, the less you will have to do at the production stage.

✔ KEYPOINTS

■ Templates must be used to ensure consistency of style

■ Follow the system of Preferences, Master Pages, H&Js, Style Sheets and Colours

METHOD OF WORKING

Preferences. This sets up the method of measuring, rules, placing of guides and various options available. In certain programs, such as QuarkXPress, these preferences also cover such controls as baseline grids, greeking and picture imports.

Master Pages. Including new page features, this covers such things as margins, folios, auto-numbering, grids, rules; in fact, anything that repeats itself throughout the publication.

H & Js. Stands for hyphenation and justification. I think it is the most critical part of the typesetting process. Design stands or falls by this vital set-up. Take your time and try various settings. You will read more on this particular feature later.

Style Sheets. Here you build up your type styles for body copy, headlines, captions and so forth, complete with formatting and tabbing if necessary. All you have to do when these are set up is highlight text and apply the style. Remember to use the style palette or keystroke macro to apply these styles. Make the computer do the work!

Colours. Mix up your shades and tints in the colour palette and apply at 100% on the page. Don't use tints of tints. This has very important colour repro implications.

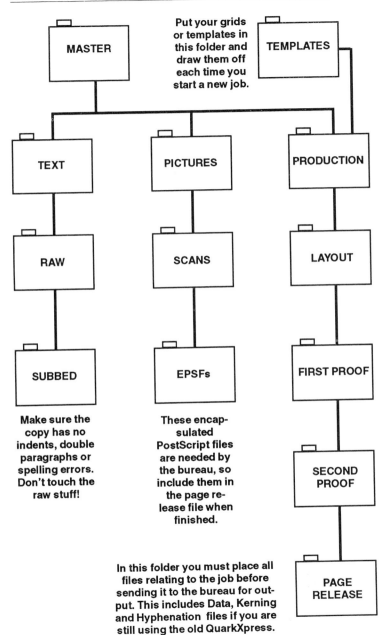

Put your grids or templates in this folder and draw them off each time you start a new job.

Make sure the copy has no indents, double paragraphs or spelling errors. Don't touch the raw stuff!

These encapsulated PostScript files are needed by the bureau, so include them in the page release file when finished.

In this folder you must place all files relating to the job before sending it to the bureau for output. This includes Data, Kerning and Hyphenation files if you are still using the old QuarkXpress.

FILE MANAGEMENT

This is an area that can cause many problems for the inexperienced operator. If poor filing is carried out, double filing and lost work and time will result. There is nothing more frustrating, when you have to take over a job from another operator, to find that they use gobbledegook for file names and have no form of structure in their filing. Are you laying out subbed or un-subbed copy? Have the illustrations been done? At what stage is the production process?

I have developed over the years a method of filing that is simple and functional. If you insist that you and all your colleagues follow this system or a version of it, work will be much easier to control. It is based on a simple job-bag system where all the elements of a job are put in one folder or file. Every job can then be planned and checked with ease and any missing parts show up quickly. It is also a boon at the page release stage, as the operator can simply find all the documents that the bureau will need for output.

This set-up is specifically designed for Macintosh users, but it applies equally to PC-type operators.

Finally, keep your files down in size; don't go above two or three pages per document. I know all the application manufacturers say that their programs can handle hundreds of pages in any document, but take my advice: use one, two or three maximum. The reason is simple – if anything goes wrong and the computer writes a bad file name for example, you have only lost a couple of pages, not the whole of *War and Peace*.

HYPHENATION AND JUSTIFICATION

I consider this to be the most important part of good typesetting in the desktop environment. Many designers, quite rightly, denigrate desktop typesetting by holding up lousy examples and saying how they can always tell it from traditional methods. Unfortunately, this is often true; the basic defaults on page make-up programs are lousy. They have to cater for Joe Public and therefore put in very basic settings on the typesetting features. However, this does not mean we cannot adjust them in a professional manner; in fact, we must.

The biggest fault lies in the spacing of type and this is controlled by the hyphenation tables and the hyphenation zone. All good page make-up programs contain pretty comprehensive hyphenation dictionaries. These contain thousands of words which not only can be checked for spelling errors but also feature hyphenation breaks – in other words, each word has a suggested breaking point which the computer will use as a hyphenation point at the end of a line if necessary.

The user adjustable part of the H&J tables firstly concerns the hyphenation zone. This is an imaginary strip down the right-hand side of the column of text and has a default of, say, 12mm. What this means is that when the line of text, justified or ranged left, reaches the line it can start looking for a hyphenation break in the dictionaries. Obviously, this is done at unbelievable speed and results in various hyphens appearing in the text. By increasing the zone to, say, 15mm you will decrease the number of options in word breaks; if you decrease it to 5mm you will increase the number.

Remember – it is better to break words than increase spacing.

The whole point of these tables is to stop the program adding spacing between words and letters to fill out a line. Given a choice, the computer will go for the simplest option and that is to *pad it out with white!* This results in the unsightly typesetting the designers moan about. To avoid these gaps that you can drive a truck through, you must next adjust the letter and word spacing. Now, this depends very much on your taste and the typeface and column width you are using. I will, however, give you some rules of thumb to work with.

Type is affected by the amount of copy to be fitted into the piece. As this is sometimes crucial, in the past a designer had to spend hours laboriously 'casting off' copy to make it fit. Now with DTP, a designer can, by trial and error, change the copy instantly on the page. It is, however, useful to know the different sizes of type and how they will fill a space. With experience, a designer can look at some copy and gauge by eye what size it should be, instinctively.

This is the same piece of copy, ranged left, but the top one is using a 5mm hyphenation zone and the lower one a 15mm zone. Notice the way the lines break with no hyphens at all in the lower one because the options to break have been cut back by allowing more line returns.

Type is affected by the amount of copy to be fitted into the piece. As this is sometimes crucial, in the past a designer had to spend hours laboriously 'casting off' copy to make it fit. Now with DTP, a designer can, by trial and error, change the copy instantly on the page. It is, however, useful to know the different sizes of type and how they will fill a space. With experience, a designer can look at some copy and gauge by eye what size it should be, instinctively.

Word Spacing

Minimum 85%   Optimum 85%   Maximum 95%

This constrains the amount of spacing the program can put between the words on a line. It also ties in with the H&J tables, each referring to the other in the search for a good place to break. Nowadays, people are used to seeing justified type and will therefore accept a certain amount of word spacing – but only about 10%. The defaults used on the programs are often as much as 25-50%! The constraint stops those nasty large gaps you see on some lines.

Letter Spacing

Minimum 0%   Optimum 0%   Maximum 1%

These percentages relate to the amount of space allowed between letters. You will notice I only allow 1%, which is because I feel that letters have been created by font designers with very specific spaces between them. To add to or subtract from these delicate gaps is sacrilege, the mark of a philistine. Keep it tiny.

Method of Working

First check your column width and type face and size. Next decide if you are ranging left or justifying the type. Now set your hyphenation zone. Next set up your spacing tables and set a column of actual text and run it out on the printer. Look for rivers and gappy lines. Adjust the zone accordingly. (QuarkXpress has added features that may be changed, such as Flush Zones – the method of pulling out a final line in a paragraph – and word hyphenation definitions.) Continue to run out proofs until you are satisfied with the feel of the text.

This procedure is worth spending a lot of time on, as it gives your setting that professional feel rather than the 'Parish Magazine' look.

The final process is to go through the text and break by hand, using soft returns and hyphens where you feel a line still looks ugly. A 'soft return/hyphen' is one which will disappear when the text is taken back for any reason, unlike a 'hard hyphen', which will stick to its word regardless. Look up the keystrokes in your manual.

Type is affected by the amount of copy to be fitted into the piece. As this is sometimes crucial, in the past a designer had to spend hours laboriously 'casting off' copy to make it fit. Now with DTP, a designer can, by trial and error, change the copy instantly on the page. It is, however, useful to know the different sizes of type and how they will fill a space. With experience, a designer can look at some copy and gauge by eye what size it should be, instinctively.

The text above has hyphenation off and default spacing of words and letters. Below is my suggested setting for H&Js. I feel the latter has a more pleasing feel to it – not perfect yet, but a good starting point. The one above has enormous variation of spacing with some letters almost touching.

Type is affected by the amount of copy to be fitted into the piece. As this is sometimes crucial, in the past a designer had to spend hours laboriously 'casting off' copy to make it fit. Now with DTP, a designer can, by trial and error, change the copy instantly on the page. It is, however, useful to know the different sizes of type and how they will fill a space. With experience, a designer can look at some copy and gauge by eye what size it should be, instinctively.

DTP

Type is affected by the amount of copy to be fitted into the piece. As this is sometimes crucial, in the past a designer had to spend hours laboriously 'casting off' copy to make it fit. Now with DTP, a designer can, by trial and error, change the copy instantly on the page. It is, however, useful to know the different sizes of type and how they will fill a space. With experience, a designer can look at some copy and gauge b should be, instinctively.

Left is some text set on *Auto*. This is 11 point on 13 point leading or 11/13. Easy on the eye.

Below, I have set it on a tighter line space - 11 point type on 11 point or 11/11. Slightly too tight but shows the effect.

DTP

Type is affected by the amount of co the piece. As this is sometimes crucial, in the past a designer had to spend hours laboriously 'casting off' copy to make it fit. Now with DTP, a designer can, by trial and error, change the copy instantly on the page. It is, however, useful to know the different sizes of type and how they will fill a space. With experience, a designer can look at some copy and gauge by eye what size it should be, instinctively.

DTP

Type is affected by the amount of copy to be fitted into the piece. As this is sometimes crucial, in the past a designer had to spend hours laboriously 'casting off' copy to make it fit. Now with DTP, a designer can, by trial and error, change the copy instantly on the page. It is, however, useful to know the different sizes of type and how they will fill a space. With experience, a designer can look at some copy and gauge by eye what size it should be, instinctively.

We see above, the effect of more line space. It makes the lines float. This is 11/18 point.

DTP

Type is affected by the amount of copy to be fitted into the piece. As this is sometimes crucial, in the past a designer had to spend hours laboriously 'casting off' copy to make it fit. Now with DTP, a

Extreme leading of 11 point on 22 point spacing, not advised unless a special style is required.

Below New Century is set in standard 11 point on Auto leading.

DTP

Type is affected by the amount of copy to be fitted into the piece. As this is sometimes crucial, in the past a designer had to spend hours laboriously 'casting off' copy to make it fit. Now with DTP, a designer can, by trial and error, change the copy instantly on the page. It is, however, useful

TYPE

Type is affected by the amount of copy to be fitted into the piece. As this is sometimes crucial, in the past a designer had to spend hours laboriously 'casting off' copy to make it fit. Casting off requires an accurate character count. The simplest way of doing this is to measure the line with a standard inch ruler, the average typewriter sets about 10-12 characters per inch, so you now multiply the number of inches by 10-12 then multiply the number of lines in the text to get the total number of characters. Then you can compare the number you have calculated with tables of type and find the size of the type that will allow the copy to fit.

However, with DTP, a designer can, by trial and error, change the copy on the page. It is, though, useful to know the different sizes of type and how they will fill a space. With experience, a designer can look at some copy and gauge by eye what size it should be, instinctively.

With modern page make-up systems the old difficult job of run arounds,making type fit around a shape, is almost instant and can enhance many design jobs. We'll look at these later. The old labour of tracing roughs and layouts are a thing of the past, as you can now work straight on the page.

Weight and shade of type

All our blocks of type have weight and shade, this is due to the choice of face and leading, letter-spacing and whether the type is bold, italic or light. Different typefaces and styles give the page a texture or colour that can be adjusted to suit the particular effect you are trying to acheive. We'll leave the individual faces for the moment and concentrate on leading, spacing and style.

✔CHECKLIST

Different faces and styles give the page a texture

Consider whether the space must be filled or will the type block float

White space is as important as the black type

Leading

Named after the strips of lead that used to separate lines of text when loose type setting was used. Leading will affect the tonal colour of the text by varying the amount of white space; it can be used to fine tune the shade of text blocks.

Letter and Word Spacing

This is the space between letters which gives another method of changing overall tonal colour. Spacing is usually influenced by line length and alters the readability of text, so be careful. Varying degrees of tonal colour can be acheived by increasing or decreasing the white showing between letters and words as you can see in the examples. Most DTP systems allow a considerable degree of letterspacing — spacing between characters.

With any text you must beware of 'rivers', these are areas of white which run in a noticeable pattern through any block of text unless care is taken over letter/word spacing. It is sometimes found in newspapers and magazines but should be avoided in any quality setting. Have a look for these white ribbons next time you look through your morning newspaper and you'll see what I mean.

Ranging Type

The next important way of changing the tonal value of a body of text is by ranging the type. This means anchoring the lines left, right or centred and justified or hyphenated. Each plays a unique part in the weight and shape of body type. The width of the setting plays an important part in this, as you can see flicking through any magazine or newspaper. See how the type shape varies and whether you think it works.

DTP

Type is affected by the amount of copy to be fitted into the piece. As this is sometimes crucial, in the past a designer had to spend hours laboriously 'casting off' copy to make it fit. Now with DTP, a designer can, by trial and error, change the copy instantly on the page. It is, however, useful to know the different sizes of type and how they will fill a space. With experience, a designer can look at some copy and gauge by eye what size it should be,

Above, some text has been set with a minimum of 50% and maximum of 200% for 9/11 point type.

Below, this time it's 9/10 point type at 300% maximum and beneath it 400% maximum. The changes are very slight but on a total page very noticeable.

Type is affected by the amount of copy to be fitted into the piece. As this is sometimes crucial, in the past a designer had to spend hours laboriously 'casting off' copy to make it fit. Now with DTP, a designer can, by trial and error, change the copy instantly on the page. It is, however, useful to know the different sizes of type and how they will fill a space. With experience, a designer can look at some copy and gauge by eye what size it should be, instinctively.

Type is affected by the amount of copy to be fitted into the piece. As this is sometimes crucial, in the past a designer had to spend hours laboriously 'casting off' copy to make it fit. Now with DTP, a designer can, by trial and error, change the copy instantly on the page. It is, however, useful to know the different sizes of type and how they will fill a space. With experience, a designer can look at some copy and gauge by eye what size it should be, instinctively.

DTP

Type is affected by the amount of copy to be fitted into the piece. As this is sometimes crucial, in the past a designer had to spend hours laboriously 'casting off' copy to make it fit. Now with DTP, a designer can, by trial and error, change the copy instantly on the page. It is, however, useful to know the different sizes of type and how they will fill a space. With experience, a designer can look at some copy and gauge by eye what size it should be, instinctively.

I T C A N L O O K V E R Y T R E N D Y T O O V E R S P A C E B U T C A R E M U S T B E T A K E N N O T T O M A K E I T I L L E G I B L E

Above is letter spaced 80% and an example of extraspaced lettering. Below is 100% spaced. All you can do is experiment and feel the differences adding letter and word spacing make to the page.

DTP

Type is affected by the amount of copy to be fitted into the piece. As this is sometimes crucial, in the past a designer had to spend hours laboriously 'casting off' copy to make it fit. Now with DTP, a designer can, by trial and error, change the copy instantly on the page. It is, however, useful to know the different sizes of type and how they will fill a space. With experience, a designer can look at some copy and gauge by eye what size it should be, instinctively.

Type is affected by the amount of copy to be fitted into the piece. As this is sometimes crucial, in the past a designer had to spend hours laboriously 'casting off' copy to make it fit. Now with DTP, a designer can, by trial and error, change the copy instantly on the page. It is, however, useful to know the different sizes of type and how they will fill a space. With experience, a

Type is affected by the amount of copy to be fitted into the piece. As this is sometimes crucial, in the past a designer had to spend hours laboriously 'casting off' copy to make it fit. Now with DTP, a designer can, by trial and error, change the copy instantly on the page. It is, however, useful to know the different sizes of type and how they will

Finally we show the different ways of ranging type. Top, ranged left, next is justified. Beneath is ranged right and finally centred. Remember, different positioning on the page will effect the way you range the type.

Type is affected by the amount of copy to be fitted into the piece. As this is sometimes crucial, in the past a designer had to spend hours laboriously 'casting off' copy to make it fit. Now with DTP, a designer can, by trial and error, change the copy instantly on the page. It is, however, useful to know the different sizes of type and how

Type is affected by the amount of copy to be fitted into the piece. As this is sometimes crucial, in the past a designer had to spend hours laboriously 'casting off' copy to make it fit. Now with DTP, a designer can, by trial and error, change the copy instantly on the page. It is, however, useful to know the different sizes of type and how they will fill a

KERNING

Each letter has white space either side. As this can look ugly in some letter combinations, it can be increased or lessened, either collectively or singly, by using the kerning program. See the effect on Te or Pa.

Te

The letters 'Te' are interesting because of the ledge effect of the arm of the T.

Te

Here I have tucked the 'e' too far under the arm of the 'T'.

Te

This spacing is just about right.

Pa

The same situation occurs with another letter combination — 'Pa'

Pa

This, again, is too close so open it out a fraction...

Pa

...and you get a much better balance

AW

Finally, here we have another problem, this time the two letters can be way out as here...

AW

...or too close. As you see this combination could even touch they are so parallel.

AW

This is just about the optimum kerning for this pair although it really depends on the following and preceding characters. They make for the overall balance.

Most DTP systems nowadays have very sophisticated automatic kerning but you will find that headlines and large type will benefit from a little individual attention.

TYPESIZE

In the past, designers had to 'cast off' using character counts and line lengths to measure exactly the font size and leading required to fill that area. With the advent of DTP, however, the designer can carry text from the word processing package into the make-up program and vary the type size to quickly make up the page. Try to use the time saved to improve on design though. I always do as much editing and sizing in the WP package. This is quicker than using the page make-up program. When you have completely finished editing the raw copy then go into the makeup program.

Here you design your grid and position any images and headlines, then, when this is done, place the text. If the result is displeasing — start again. It will only take a minute to re-make a grid, so save under one file name and start again. Don't be afraid to experiment; you have the tools with the power and the speed.

To check the page you can squint. By out-of-focussing your eyes deliberately, you eliminate all unnecessary details and see the page as shapes and tones. I call this the 'designer squint', In this way you will get a much clearer idea of the value of your design.

Lorem ipsum dolor sit amet, consectetuer adipiscing elit, sed diam nonummy nibh euismod tincidunt ut laoreet dolore magna aliquam erat volutpat. Ut wisi enim ad minim veniam, quis nostrud exerci tation ullamcorper suscipit lobortis nisl ut aliquip ex ea commo consequat. Duis autem vel eum iriure dolor in hendrerit in vulputate velit esse molestie consequat, vel illum dolore eu feugiat nulla facilisis at vero eros et accumsan et iusto odio dignissim qui blandit praesent luptatum zzril delenit augue duis dolore te feugait nulla facilisi. Lorem ipsum dolor sit amet, consectetuer adipiscing elit, sed diam nonummy nibh euismod tincidunt ut laoreet dolore magna aliquam erat volutpat. Ut wisi enim ad minim veniam, quis nostrud exerci tation ullamcorper suscipit lobortis nisl ut aliquip ex ea commodo consequat.

Duis autem vel eum iriure dolor in hendrer in vulputate velit esse molestie consequat, vel illum dolore eu feugiat nulla facilisis at vero eros et accumsan et iusto e feugait nulla facilisi. Nam liber tempor cum soluta nobis eleifend option congue nihil imperdiet doming id quod mazim placerat facer possim assum. Lorem ipsum dolor sit amet, consectetuer adipiscing elit, sed diam nonummy nibh euismod tincidunt ut laoreet dolore magna aliquam erat volutpat. Ut wisi enim ad minim veniam, quis

✔ KEYPOINTS

Write in a word processing package — it uses less memory and sub there too, if possible.

Used the time saved to improve the design.

Use your 'designer squint'

A column of various sized text from 14, 12, 10, 9, 8 and 6 point shows you roughly how they feel between a column's width. It's a keystroke to change it, so experiment!

CROSSHEADS

Check any newspaper and see how these, apparently random, lines occur in long columns of text. They act as a metaphorical bench for the weary eyes to rest and catch their breath before setting off refreshed on to the next block of type. Basically there are two kinds of crosshead, the rule and the sub-heading. A rule can be a basic box or a tint or solid black. A subhead is useful for the added reason that it acts as a signpost which lets the reader know where they are in the text.

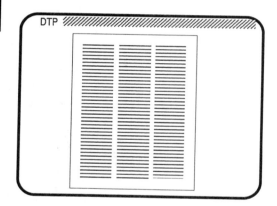

A page of text like this one above is dull and unrelenting but below it is relieved by some crossheads placed in the design.

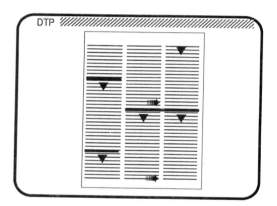

These cross heads act as directional markers, too, helping the readers to find their way. Some examples of styles are shown below.

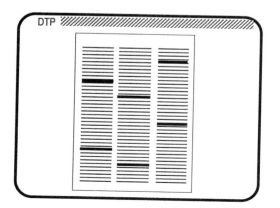

Heavy Rule

Open Rules

Closed Rules

Sub-Heading   **Latest Consideration**

The Mark Twain Heritage Centre

On a spread, remember you can sometimes use all the page . When there is not too much text then blow up and bleed the image and try run-rounds and reversals. Take care with colour reversals, mind the text doesn't get lost.

✔KEYPOINTS

Crossheads act as a resting place for the eyes

They also decorate an otherwise dull column of text

If actual words are used, they act as signposts

TYPEFACES

A character is a means of communication. It is part of the whole word which, in turn, is part of the tone of the whole page area. So, initially, think of letters as portions of a picture. Letters can be divided into two main distinct groups, serif and sans serif.

Serif. These are the sort of letters with curly bits on the end like tails. They were derived from the chiselled faces the Roman masons used on their monuments. The faces are great for body copy and you will find most books and magazines set in this style. The reason being that the serifs give the eye a natural link, letter to letter, rather like joined-up writing, and help the eye to hop to the next character quickly and easily.

Sans Serif. These faces have no tails and are more modern in feeling, coming into use mainly in the 20th Century. The text you are reading now is set in a sans serif face. I feel it works mainly because the blocks of text are not over large, therefore the eye doesn't get fatigued too quickly. Sans serif faces are simple in construction and can take any amount of letter spacing. This facility makes them popular for use in headlines where a space must be filled by a few words.

Serif

Serif faces are conservative in general, the tails or serifs give an old fashioned flavour to the face. This is Times 48pt.

Sans Serif

The sans serif face is plainer, more modern but not so simple for the eye to follow. This is Avant Garde 48pt.

✔ KEYPOINTS

Letters are the texture makers of the page picture

Serif letters are fancy — Sans Serif are plain

Earliest letters were drawn by pen hence the thick and thin lines on many faces

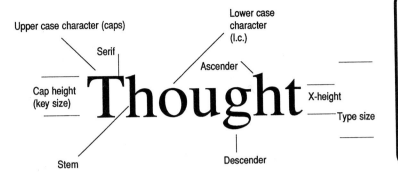

Upper case character (caps)
Serif
Lower case character (l.c.)
Ascender
Cap height (key size)
X-height
Type size
Stem
Descender

Thought

DTP

Pens developed the first letters

Early type was based on calligraphic script.

The first type faces in common usage were drawn by pen hence the noticeable thick and thin ascenders and descenders in a letter of the old style.

These stems and arms are what give a typeface its style and clarity. It is a very fine difference in most faces but it enhances the contrast of the texture on the page.

MATCHING THE FACE TO THE JOB

The first consideration about type is to choose the typeface which will suit the job. There is no point in setting a funeral parlour price list in a jolly style. So consider your audience, the impression you are trying to give and the practicality of legibility. The amount of space available is also important: how much do you have to fit in the given area? Does it affect the overall design?

As a general rule, avoid large sizes in body copy. It looks crude and clumsy and, worst of all, looks as though you are trying to fill up the area as there isn't enough copy! So choose around 9- to 12- point sizes and experiment with leading and so on. Thanks to the wonders of DTP this is so simple now you can afford to try a couple of treatments on a job without taking much more time.

DTP

SWEET NOTHINGS
Florist Shops and Rental

Choose a face that fits. A flower shop does not want a block sans serif type, use something more flowery.

DTP

SWEET NOTHINGS
Florist Shops and Rental

Once you have decided on a face, stick to it. Only use another face with care and for emphasis. Avoid mixing faces of a similar type, sans serif with sans serif and serif with serif as the styles are too similar to be comfortable.Look how this sans serif face, called Avant Garde, clashes with the Helvetica above.

Remember, type is part of a word which is part of a line, which is part of a paragraph and it is basically a series of lines with white space between. The white space defines clarity and legibility.

Once you have decided on a face, stick to it. Only use another face with care and for emphasis. Avoid mixing faces of a similar type, sans serif with sans serif and serif with serif as the styles are too similar to be comfortable.

Captions should be a smaller size than the body copy but can, in turn, be emboldened. Captions are usually read prior to the body copy, The usual path of reading is

- Headline
- Picture
- Caption
- Text

Therefore a resumé can be usefully put in a picture caption to make the reader want to know more.

Introductions can be treated in the same way, that is to say change face, embolden, but this time you should enlarge the type size. Again, we're trying to drag the customer off the street so the intro must be snappy and witty to interest the reader. If emphasis in the text is required we are able to call on other means in the typesetter's arsenal.

Captions can be treated in various ways. This is emboldened italic.

Or you could try a thinner face, up a size.

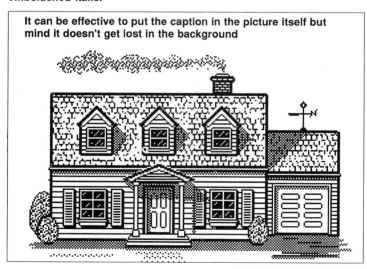

It can be effective to put the caption in the picture itself but mind it doesn't get lost in the background

Put in a tint box like this

Reverse it out of a black box

HOW DOES ① THE EYE TRAVEL?

Amazing new facts bring to light a ③ ole new area of endeavour

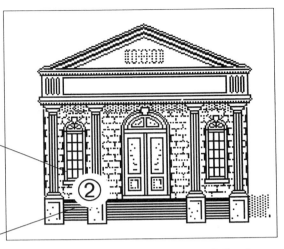

Quia uis magnast ipsus, et alte aera per purum grauter simulcra ferunter, et feriunt oculus ⑤ ntia compositus. Preatera splendor quicumque est acer adurit saepa oculus, ideo quod semina. Urida preatera fiunt tuentur arqutrie quia luroris de compore eonum semina multa fluent simulcris.

Quia uis magnast ipsus, et alte aera per purum grauter simulcra ferunter, et feriunt oculus turbantia compositus. Preatera splendor quicumque est acer adurit saepa oculus, ideo quod semina.

The vision of one man has changed the face of type. He dis④ ed that the eye moves across the pag④ ir with the added serif.

Urida preatera fiunt tuentur arqutrie quia luroris de compore eonum semina multa fluent simulcris.Quia uis magnast ipsus, et alte aera per purum grauter simulcra ferunter, et feriunt oculus turbantia compositus.

Preatera splendor quicumque est acer adurit saepa oculus, ideo quod semina. Urida preatera fiunt tuentur arqutrie quia luroris de compore eonum semina multa fluent simulcris.Quia uis magnast ipsus, et alte aera per purum grauter simulcra ferunter, et feriunt oculus turbantia compositus. Preatera splendor quicumque est

If you look at this page of an article you will see how your eye moves from one element to the next

EMPHASIS

We can bring out a salient point very easily in a body of copy by the following devices.

Bold. This is the thickening of the lines of a letter. It doesn't change a letter's size but just its weight, therefore changing the colour of a paragraph considerably - but that is the whole point.

Italic. A more delicate way of emphasising a word or phrase. Can be difficult to read on screen in WYSIWYG.

Underline. Basic rule under a word or sentence. I recommend not using this method in DTP as the rule usually cuts through the descenders of the letters and looks terrible.

CAPITAL LETTERS (Caps) The most fundamental way of stressing type.

SMALL CAPS. An interesting style this, very good for handling qualifications after someone's name. Make sure your machine does proper small caps and not just a smaller type size.

Shadow Only useful in headlines, really. Also the tone used to indicate the shadow does not print well in some cases.

The *use* of various styles of emphasis **must** be considered CAREFULLY as <u>over use</u> tends to *devalue* its impact. Little and special is the rule.

Shadowed text in this case is better, it is a gimmick and should be used as such - not within body copy.

DTP

leader 'communicates' that will ensure a secure environment conducive to learning. An environment that will motivate staff development and a building of good relationships within the school network. It can be seen then that **Interpersonal** skills are of paramount importance to a leader

Shadowed emphasis is too emphatic.

DTP

Albert Einstein, FRS, MSc, ASCAP
PROFESSOR OF HIGHER MATHEMATICS

Best use of Small Caps, they give the qualifications their own identity without being overpowering.

DTP

TWENTIETH CENTURY
MONUMENTS

✔ KEYPOINTS

■ Use emphasis styles sparingly

■ The letter is the basic building block of text

■ Legibility is the basis of good design

Heads must be aware that they are serving the individual (the child) and society; and what is more, school 'managers' operate in a very public area. Leadership is by its very nature influencing people. The school 'manager' is influencing staff to ensure maximum efficiency and effectiveness of teaching. Therefore communication at all levels is a desirable attribution of a leader. **The Head of a school is at the centre of a communication network. These groups will influence the head teacher as he is seen as the focal point of the school, but he or she, in turn, needs to ensure communications between the groups.** The Head has an overview and from the various points of view is expected to form a School Policy - curriculum, ethos etc. which are then communicated to all the groups who form the school network. It is the way the

The emboldened sentence in this example gives it extra weight, which tends to change the whole text block. Try the 'designer's squint.'

You can see in this example, how italic type highlights the particular sentence in a pleasing way without altering the weight of the text dramatically.

Then throughout the 1970s a large number of colleges and universities established qualifications in education management. This official recognition of the importance of school management promoted research and a reawakening amongst educationists to looking seriously at industry for possible pointers to development among head teachers. *In the past there has been a tendency for Business to ascribe the problems of schools to the incompetence of educators and for educators to see business as concerned only with profits.* As the role of the leader/manager is now changing to encompass direction and budgeting of finances, managing curriculum changes, both national and in special educational needs; parent partnership, staff development and motivating the staff to meet these changes in a positive and co-operative way, it is obvious that many skills and a continual up-to-date knowledge of education is required. So schools need to be seen as professional, accountable and yet retain their prime motive which is

Computer typefaces

DTP has revolutionised typesetting by making it available to all. However, technology outstripped typography in the early days and system developers seemed to be more interested in mixing text and graphics than dealing with typefaces so we had a lousy initial selection. The Macintosh had Courier, Geneva, Monaco, New York, Chicago and, thankfully ,Times and Helvetica. But these were mostly 'screen faces'. This meant they were designed for good legibility on screen but were appalling when printed. Typefaces that are designed simply for computer screens have a very low resolution of only 72 dots per inch. This means that when they are printed on high resolution printing devices, such as a laser printer, the rough edges of the characters can be seen quite distinctly.

DTP ///////////////////////////////////////

Lorem ipsum dolor sit amet, consectetuer adipiscing elit, sed diam nonummy nibh euismod tincidunt ut laoreet dolore magna aliquam erat volutpat. Ut wisi enim ad minim veniam, quis nostrud exerci tation ullamcorper

This is a computer screen face called Chicago, it looks fine on screen but prints very badly.

This is another face, called Geneva, again a screen face mimicking Helvetica.

DTP //

suscipit lobortis nisl ut aliquip ex ea commodo consequat. Duis autem vel eum iriure dolor in hendrerit in vulputate velit esse molestie consequat, vel illum dolore eu feugiat nulla facilisis at vero eros et accumsan et iusto odio dignissim qui blandit praesent luptatum zzril delenit

ADOBETYPE

✔ KEYPOINTS
■ The reader's eye must not become lost
■ There are no hard and fast rules — only guidelines

What's Available?

The average DTP system comes with several basic faces already loaded, just to get you started. There are, however, hundreds of fonts available from the font manufacturers. Every week sees some new releases, many being especially designed with DTP in mind. Adobe has been producing PostScript faces since its conception, but now type houses such as Linotype, Monotype and Bitstream are almost exclusively producing digital fonts and the quality is superb. Now you can even design your own digital fonts with applications like Fontographer, creating exciting new styles and making them into actual typefaces. Tricky, but worthwhile.

You need two kinds of font with a desktop computer, the screen font and the printer font. The screen font is a bitmap and is loaded deep into the system itself, while the printer font is an outline font and best left open in the system folder. Suitcase II is a useful utility which allows font suitcases to be opened and closed as necessary; otherwise the font menu can seem endless and the system itself can be overloaded.

I suggest you contact any of the above type houses or a reputable distributor such as FontWorks and ask for a catalogue. Your dealer should have a comprehensive listing as well.

This is 12 point Aachen, Bold, Italic and Outline

This is 12 point Garamond Medium, Bold, Italic and **Outline**

This is 12 point Franklin Gothic Demi, **Bold**, *Italic* and Outline

This is 12 point Helvetica Medium, **Bold**, *Italic* and Outline

This is 12 point Futura **Bold**, *Italic* and Outline

*This is 12 point Seville Medium, **Bold**, Italic and Outline*

This is 12 point Kabel Medium, **Bold,** *Italic* and Outline

This is 12 point Times Medium, **Bold,** *Italic* and Outline

THIS IS 12 POINT STENCIL BOLD, ITALIC AND OUTLINE

Not all these faces will be on your system, some will be — but under such names as Dutch and Swiss. Many beautiful faces are available from suppliers and are easy to install and use. Just follow the instructions.

Special Effects. For a reasonable price it is possible to buy software which will stretch or condense your existing typefaces – placing far more faces at your disposal and enabling you to fill a given area by manipulation. A very modern technique, it has been used to stunning effect in some recent magazine designs. It is worth while studying this approach to see the exciting results you can get from stretching letters to almost unreadable levels. But proceed with caution; type designers have spent years developing beautifully proportioned letters with specific widths and strokes and the computer can – and does – distort these critical thicks and thins, creating in most cases ugly shapes. Use the actual cut of the face where possible.

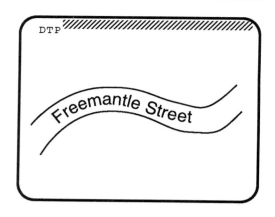

Columns. They need not be the same size across the page. A rough guide is 8 words or 50 characters per line, so if you have a small face you can get away with narrow columns. Larger type must have a wider measure, otherwise hyphenation becomes problematic.

Columns. They need not be the same size across the page. A rough guide is 8 words or 50 characters per line, so if you have a small face you can get away with narrow columns. Larger type must have a wider measure, otherwise hyphenation becomes problematic.

Columns. They need not be the same size across the page. A rough guide is 8 words or 50 characters per line, so if you have a small face you can get away with narrow columns. Larger type must have a wider measure, otherwise hyphenation becomes problematic – see?

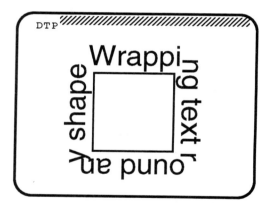

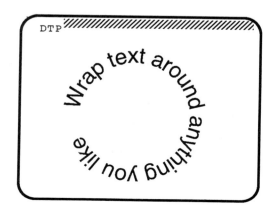

I have made up some text shapes in a drawing program to show how type can be simply made to follow a shape or line. Top right is a way of naming a road or river. Next two screens show a fancy wrap round a circle shape and a square. The possibilities are enormous with DTP. Above you can see how small type seems OK but larger type looks cramped across a narrow measure.

Pull Pull

Pull

Pull

Pull

Pull

Pull

Above are some treatments of words in a drawing package which can be transferred to the page make-up program as encapsulated PostScript files (EPSFs) when manipulation is completed.

Here you can see a serif and sans serif character being condensed and expanded. Not recommended as this deforms the delicate design of the face. Use sparingly.

M M M M M M M

Serif character widths set to 70%, 80%, 90%, 100%, 110%, 120%, 130%

M M M M M M M

Sans Serif character widths set to 70%, 80%, 90%, 100%, 110%, 120%, 130%

IMAGES

After type, the other main elements in any document or design are images. An image is anything that is not a word. It could be a letter, such as a decorative capital, but I define images as photographs, illustrations, maps, charts, graphs, motifs, logos, diagrams or even dingbats such as blobs and triangles.

Blocks of type can be attractive but images are the real sparkle to a page. It is a great truth that a picture speaks a thousand words, why do you think all traffic signs are pictograms? The eye and brain can assimilate an enormous amount of information instantly with a picture, no matter how simple it is. Images are also international. People from Australia and China understand exactly the same picture, because no words are used, or are necessary.

But how do we use images in DTP? The first thing you must realise is that many images takes up a large amount of memory on the computer. Each line or dot has to be calculated mathematically.

Photographs. These constitute a large part of designs in advertising, magazines and brochures and can be handled in two ways. Firstly they can be scanned in and placed on the computer page to be run out with the text, or space may be left in the computer page and then pasted into the spaces.

This strip shows the various line effects obtainable in Quark Xpress, all on a 20 dot line screen to coarsen up the scanned image and make the differences more obvious.
Top to bottom - dot, line, ellipse square.

Illustrations. In much the same way as photographs, these may be scanned in and then manipulated in a drawing package. Alternatively, they may be generated completely within the the computer. As drawing packages become more sophisticated, the latter option seems to be preferable. Some incredible work is now achieved using these art packages and, as more artists use the medium, so the output will improve. Another useful option is the library disk. This is a piece of software like a scrapbook which you can browse through and cut out the picture or image you require, to be pasted onto the page in the computer. The library disks can be used again and again and have hundreds of images you can use, saving you time.

Maps. Again these are available on commercial disks in many cases. For local areas you will have to scan-in an existing map and re-draw parts or start from scratch.

Charts & Graphs. I would recommend investing in a good graph/chart software package, it will save you hours of tedious work, slaving over a calculator. These packages will calculate the graph and draw it in any style you wish, including colours.

Diagrams. These are tricky. Sometimes you will get a finished diagram from a technical illustrator, in which case you just paste it in, sometimes it is possible to scan it in and import it, or you may get a scribble from the author and have to do the whole thing yourself. Thanks to the latest drawing packages, diagrams are very simple to produce and can be exported into the made up page within the computer.

Motifs & Logos. These may scanned in and kept on disk, if they are used frequently, or drawn specially and imported to the make-up program.

Dingbats. These are the decorative knick-knacks usually on the font disk, that can be dropped in with a key stroke and enlarged or reduced in the same manner as a single letter. They are very attractive and can give a block of text a lift but be warned — they do look a bit dated.

A typical array of dingbats

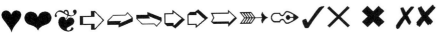

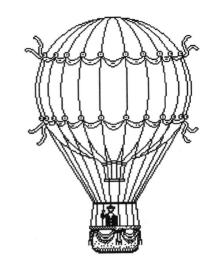

There are two ways of displaying an image in PostScript, object oriented and bitmapped. Each has definite characteristics of its own.

Object Oriented

Most drawings and illustrations that appear on a page are a result of object oriented artwork. All objects in PostScript are drawn by control points, and changing or shifting these points causes the image to change. The points are drawn by what are called Bezier curves, and they render smooth shapes around an image. Type and line art are typical examples of this form of drawing, and because the curves are drawn by formulas and algorithms they can be resized very precisely with no distortion to the image. It is also reasonably cheap in memory size to create illustrations like this.

Most drawing packages such as Freehand and Illustrator use control points with handles which act as stretching bars, infinitely bending and converting the Bezier curves in-between.

Output

High resolution imagesetters can only print dots on to film or paper and therefore convert all the elements in a document into bitmaps before they can be output. This process is called ripping or rasterising. The imagesetter has a translation device called a Raster Image Processor (RIP) between it and the input computer, which converts objects and bitmaps into machine pixels or bitmaps at a specified resolution.

The object drawing enables characters to be made into outlines, filled or distorted as you can see here.

The drawing points have handles which manipulate the Bezier curves, giving smooth lines between the points. The oval can be changed by ungrouping and twisting the handles.

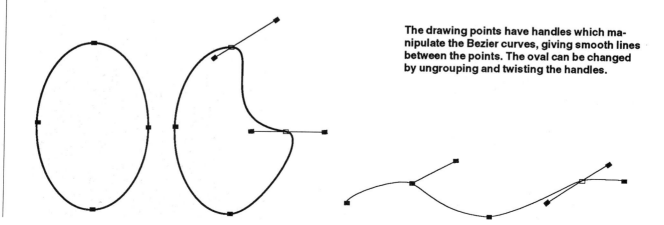

Bitmapped

These images are made up of a map of picture elements or pixels. If you imagine them to be squares like those in a crossword puzzle and in mono mode just display on or off, they require one 'bit' of information for each pixel. This will produce a burnt-out image with no greys at all.

Currently, however, graphics programs need much more detail than that. Therefore each pixel has not only to store its position on the page but also which of 256 shades of grey or colour it represents. Up to 16 million colours can be shown, but to do so the pixel must use 24 bits of information for its description.

Usually bitmaps are used to display photographic images and are converted into screens or halftones when output to the imagesetter. Here we come to the resolution factor, the number of dots or pixels to the inch. Most images are fine using 300 dots per inch (dpi), but if you go higher the computer memory and storage required can be enormous.

This is a simple bitmap, on-off. Each square takes up one bit of memory.

Here we have a greyscale of four, requiring more memory.

An eight greyscale giving more information and a smoother transition from white to black, but still pretty coarse.

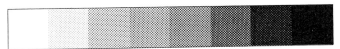

Here is a smooth degradé or graded tint. It goes through thirty changes, top to bottom.

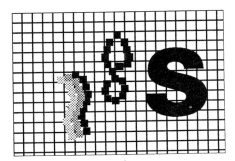

This represents a basic grid of pixels and how two-bit and greyscale pixels work. Remember they also need to know where they are on the page – rather like a map reference, four across twelve down.

SCANNING

Many graphics used in DTP are scanned in, but nowadays we can also scan in text, using 'Optical Character Recognition' (OCR) software, but first let's see what a scanner does. If you think of it vaguely as a photocopier, you have the right idea. A light is shone onto a document and the reflection is analysed and converted into a digital form in the computer. This information is then used to re-draw the image on the screen. The quality of the image depends upon the resolution of the scan which is measured in 'dots per inch' (dpi).

Scanners offer a choice of resolution, from 75dpi to up to 800dpi in some cases. With a low resolution the scan is faster. However, if you lower the resolution the the image is coarser when printed. So if you want high quality images you must be patient and use a higher resolution.

Another problem with scanners is the difficulty they have in handling halftones or photographs. Because the scanner sees everything as black and white, it finds it hard to recognise greys, so they have special software to convert greys into black and white. There are machines which will handle up to 256 different levels of grey. But how good the scanner, a laser printer will only print at 300dpi. Keep in mind also that a page of graphics will use up 1Mb of memory and a halftone can use anything up to several megabytes, so scanning is very memory expensive.

This is the sort of variation bands you can get for contrast, lines and dot adjustments. You decide accordingly on the final printout. Printed from *Quark Xpress* at 60 lines per inch with 45º screen.

✔ KEYPOINTS

■ Scanning can be more expensive that traditional methods of stripping in.

■ The lower the resolution the faster the scan and output and *vice versa*.

COLOUR SCANNING

This is major development that has occurred recently. Desktop colour scanners are extremely affordable and can give resolutions of 800dpi (or even up to 1200dpi) to both reflective artwork and transparencies. This means that photographs can be scanned and placed on the page with acceptable quality to be directly output, but they do have large memory requirements. I suggest you refer to the pixel bitmaps I discussed earlier and imagine how much more memory is required to describe a coloured pixel. Picture compression is still in its early days but JPEG style software will reduce the memory size of most if not all graphics, allowing the operator to manipulate images and store and transfer files with greater speed and accuracy. Similarly, imagesetters will not be tied up for hours outputting halftones in a page.

OPTICAL CHARACTER RECOGNITION

The other area that is very exciting in scanning is OCR. This means that a page of text can be scanned and the words understood by the computer as if they had been keyed in. You will immediately realise how much time this could save, but the method is not perfected yet. The scanner looks at a letter and compares it with a dictionary of similar letters until it gets a match, then sends it to the computer. There was a time when certain typefaces and styles could not be read because they were not easily recognised. Now, however, virtually any face or quality can be scanned, even dot-matrix printouts.

Scanners are an expensive peripheral but, if used constantly, will repay the investment quickly. If you find, however, that you cannot justify such outlay, you can always use a bureau to scan images on to a floppy disk for you to use when you need. A major drawback with using scanned images is the time taken for printing. This could add to the costs and it may be cheaper to paste in images at the printing stage.

The way OCR software works is by looking at a letter and comparing it with the letters it holds in its dictionary. It keeps comparing until it finds a match and then saves that one. You will have to go through the document afterwards to check, as they do make mistakes — but they speed up the process of text input incredibly. You can also get translator programs that will change one system format into another.

The OCR software reads this letter and says to itself, 'It's round so it could be…'

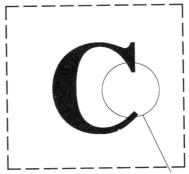

'… a 'c' — but it has not got a gap here so it might be …'

'…an 'o' but it has a little tail here so it must be a 'Q'.'

DRAWING PACKAGES

Most DTP systems have a drawing program. The early ones were rather crude but now they are remarkably sophisticated. The basic ones just draw technical graphics like flow charts, simple diagrams on so on. Expensive programs like 'Adobe Illustrator' and 'Aldus Freehand' are complicated and to get the best out of them requires a lot of training. Still, you can achieve some stunning drawings with them.

These packages will allow you to draw perfect curves and shapes thanks to a join-the-dots style of drawing, where the computer smooths the lines in-between, for you. You can also lay tints and colours and manipulate, edit or change a scanned-in image.

The other great use for these packages is their ability to manipulate type. You can set a headline and stretch it, distort it into or around any shape you like, then export it to your final design.

These are the sort of simple graphics you can manage with a drawing package.

You start off by setting and describing the face and size you require ...

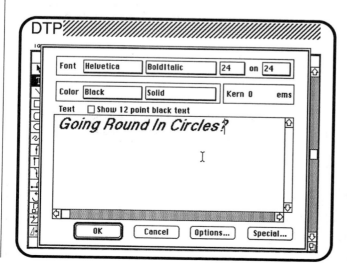

...and wrapping it round a required shape. This is a close-up to show how you can manipulate the image. Note the size of the dots at this magnification.

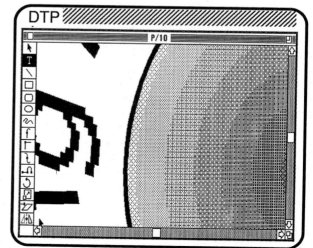

The illustration techniques on the various programs are superb, the one on the left was done in minutes. The textures and brush palettes are at the left and bottom of the screen.

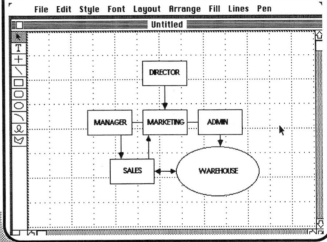

This is a classic drawing showing an organisational flow chart. In the past it would have taken hours of paste up and costly setting. Now it's a simple case of DTP at its best.

Here is the sort of standard you can get up to with a good drawing package. Stunning textures and great shapes. Try for yourself.

GRAPHS AND CHARTS

This is a vital part of DTP as the program that makes up graphs and charts is so much quicker — minutes instead of days — you will make more profit from this particular DTP skill than any other. There are various charts and graphs, the main ones being Bar, Linear, Pie, Stack, Point, Area and Polar. Each one has a particular application to specific figures so think carefully before opting for one. A pie-chart will not show an increase like a linear one, for example, but it will show a percentage far better. Also, try using depth and tints to give them a bit of texture and colour.

These are some of the graphs that you can produce with ease on DTP software. Below left is the pie chart, good for showing single figures like percentages. Right is the stack chart which shows comparisons or increases in a set of figures.

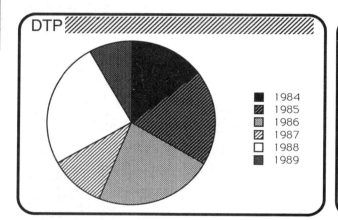

This is the area graph, it is useful for blocking in generalities and showing overall movements

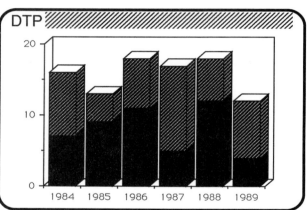

Lastly, the linear graph, a splendid way of showing several different sets of figures in relation to each other.

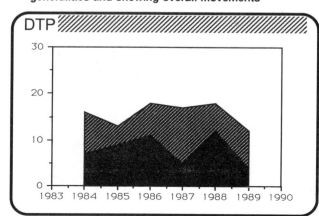

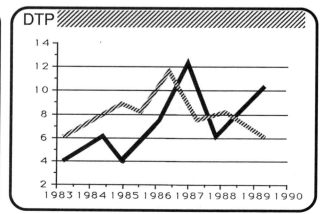

CROPPING

One last element we should consider about images is how to crop. Most DTP programs have a cropping tool which allows you to trim a photo or image to whatever proportion you like. You will often find a basic photograph, for example, is too vague in its subject matter, the eye does not know what to zoom in on — so we as designers must do it for them. Careful cropping can make a reasonable photo a stunner. We can shun the unimportant surroundings and zero in on the pertinent element with dramatic effect. We can also balance a picture better by using our judgement, making it look better on the page by increasing or decreasing the margins and centering.

Another perennial dilemma is the head shot. You will always have some director's head or personality's mug shot to position on a page so try and find a new treatment for head and shoulders. Apart from cut outs and clever cropping you can always use a scanner's facility for modifying the image from dot to line pattern.

This is a cut out with text runing round the image, a useful device for typographical shapes.

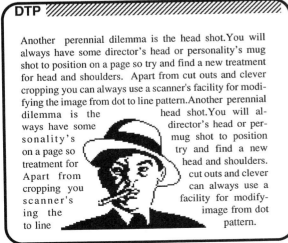

DTP

Another perennial dilemma is the head shot. You will always have some director's head or personality's mug shot to position on a page so try and find a new treatment for head and shoulders. Apart from cut outs and clever cropping you can always use a scanner's facility for modifying the image from dot to line pattern. Another perennial dilemma is the head shot. You will always have some director's head or per- sonality's mug shot to position on a page so try and find a new treatment for head and shoulders. Apart from cut outs and clever cropping you can always use a scanner's facility for modify- ing the image from dot to line pattern.

RULES, BOXES AND TINTS

Any block of text, be it a magazine page or an advertisement, can be brightened by the addition of rules, boxes and tints. Using decorative devices such as these is fine but stronger when used with a specific purpose like emphasis or colour. Before DTP these processes were fairly complex but now with the simple page make-up routines, they make a dull page come alive.

Rules

These are the thin or thick lines that divide a page, either vertically or horizontally. They organise space, and act as dividers between elements — this ends here and that starts there. Used vertically, they help to separate columns from each other. Horizontally, they open up text and headers and can lead the eye across the page. Depending on the weight of rule (thickness) texture and colour can be added. Here are some sample weights:

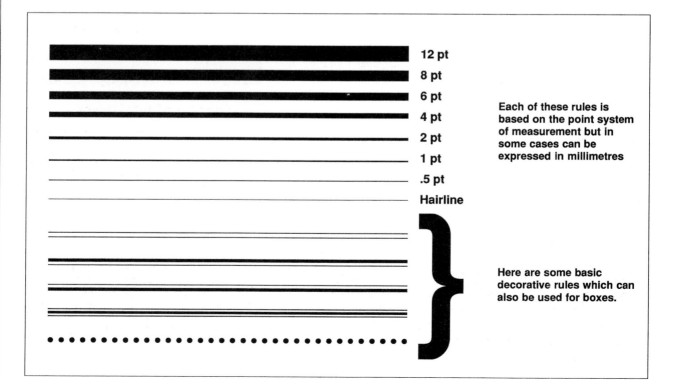

12 pt

8 pt

6 pt

4 pt

2 pt

1 pt

.5 pt

Hairline

Each of these rules is based on the point system of measurement but in some cases can be expressed in millimetres

Here are some basic decorative rules which can also be used for boxes.

Rules also form a grid or pattern for consecutive pages. Organising text or elements is vital in a complex layout. Again if we look at a newspaper we can see this organisation at its most obvious. We wouldn't know where an article began or ended, so they put rules across a column or area to make this divide obvious. Try running the rules off the page, see how the eye follows. Notice how space differs when the rule touches a box and when it stops short.

Boxes
A box encloses a special 'something'. If there is a footnote that enlarges on a piece in the text or an editorial 'aside' then this is where the box comes in. By putting a rule completely round an element, be it a picture or text block, it takes on a separate identity, it's like putting a little fence around it. It certainly brings attention to this partitioned item which is the whole intention. Notice the similarity to a picture frame, a box can be a decorative border making a little window on the page. So try various thicknesses and style of borders and notice the way this affects the balance of the page. A complete page that has been boxed has a classical look and enhances the textbook or manual design. Remember that a fence can be broken — and with great effect. Try broken boxes, where the text or image falls out of the border. Also try double overlaps, when one box lays on another, giving a 3-D effect.

You will also have to adjust the width of your text as there is nothing worse than inserting a box that is wider than the column. So trim the line width and allow a border of white within the box and all will be well. It's also acceptable to embolden or change the typeface within the box. .

You will also have to adjust the width of your text as there is nothing worse than inserting a box that is wider than the column. So trim the line width and allow a border of white within the box and all will be well. It's also acceptable to embolden or change the typeface within the box.

Coupons and cut outs are an Art in themselves. The dotted lines, or 'broken rules' as they are called, can be any weight.

The weight depends on the importance of the coupon and how much attention you want to draw to it

Again watch out that the coupon fits within the column by narrowing the type measure.

You must also change type size and style in a coupon to differentiate between it and the body copy

Try one of these scissor motifs too, they tell the reader what they must do with the coupon.

Here you can see the difference between setting the boxed text within the column width and not. As you will notice, having the box proud of the column looks like a clumsy afterthought. Allow a border of white around the text within the box.

This is a 20% tint and you can see
how text shows up against it within
a box. Urida preraeta fieunt est
tueneror arquitae quia luroris de
compredore econim
uis vertali bonum sulus id serno es

This is a 20% tint and you can see
how text shows up against it within
a box. Urida preraeta fieunt est
tueneror arquitae quia luroris de
compredore econim
uis vertali bonum sulus id serno es

This is a 30% tint and you can see
how text shows up against it within
a box. Urida preraeta fieunt est
tueneror arquitae quia luroris de
compredore econim
uis vertali bonum sulus id serno es

This is a 30% tint and you can see
how text shows up against it within
a box. Urida preraeta fieunt est
tueneror arquitae quia luroris de
compredore econim
uis vertali bonum sulus id serno es

This is a 40% tint and you can see
how text shows up against it within
a box. Urida preraeta fieunt est
tueneror arquitae quia luroris de
compredore econim
uis vertali bonum sulus id serno es

This is a 40% tint and you can see
how text shows up against it
within a box. Urida preraeta fieunt
est tueneror arquitae quia luroris
de compredore econim

Tints

These used to be the bugbear of the pre-DTP days. Paste-up or laying of tints added to the cost of a job, especially at printing stage. Now, however, the tint is there at the touch of a key.

The use of tints, as with boxes, can be the perfect substitute when there is no picture available and a page is dull. Carefully placed, they bring out a piece of text in the same way a box does but with 'colour'.

There is one problem with tints that is vital to understand. Depending on the density of the screen you can either print black text on tone (BOT) or white out of tone (WOT). Legibility suffers greatly with the intensity of screen of the tint, so be careful.

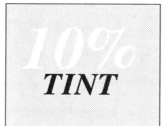

QUOTES

Another wonderful device in the designer's arsenal is the pulled quote. Again, if faced with a plain page of text and no graphic image, you can liven things up with a quote. Get the writer or sub-editor to pull out a line or two of importance from the body of text and you can then make a design feature of them. Use huge quote marks.

Try a bigger type size or different face — but make a change in the tonal quality of the design.

The way a quote is handled can be as attractive and helpful as a picture, on a page. These examples show the 'colour' and weight of a tinted quote and a straight boxed quote. There are many other ways of making them work on the page — as usual, experiment!

Quotes

QUOTES

Another wonderful device in the designer's arsenal is the pulled quote. Again, if faced with a plain page of text and no graphic image, you can liven things up with a quote. Get the writer or sub-editor to pull out a line or two of importance from the body of text and you can then make a design feature of them. Use huge quote marks. Try a bigger type size or different face — but make a change in the tonal quality of the design.

COLOUR

As we are in the business of communicating, one major aspect we must consider is colour — what it is and how to use it. Colour is probably the most powerful communicator in nature. Red, for example, sets the alarm bells ringing. Most of us see the world in full glorious colour and we are subtly under its spell throughout our lives. Once it was the artist alone who knew its secrets, but now designers of interiors and packaging, gardeners and scientists all take it into consideration when conceiving a design or environment.

The basic ways colours affect us are:

• Temperature
• Mood
• Meaning

Temperature. This is where colours get names describing their temperature, such as blues and greens are cool or cold depending on their strength, while reds, yellows and oranges generate a feeling of heat. It would be foolish to try and sell a hot new product in a cool soft pastel shade.

Mood is the impression a colour or shade gives; do you feel relaxed — often a light green has this effect — or do you feel agitated, as with yellow? The way colour can change moods is a study in itself and utilised in room decor has stunning results. Imagine sitting in a pillar-box red room or sea blue surroundings. Some colours are quiet, usually pastel shades, and can relax, or in extreme cases, actually depress the observer. Aggressive colours have the opposite effect, either startling or exciting the onlooker. Keep these points in mind when choosing colours — what sort of mood do you wish to express?

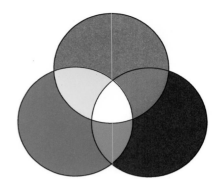

Reflected light is composed of cyan, magenta and yellow which when mixed together produces red green and blue. Here white is the absence of all colour.

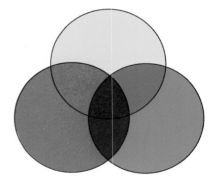

Transmitted light is made up of red, blue and green which when mixed produce cyan magenta and yellow. In this case all colours together produce grey or black depending on their intensity.

✔ KEYPOINTS

Find out how many colours you *can* use in the budget and how much you *should* use

Choose the colours most appropriate for your brief

48

Meaning. All colours have a meaning. In ancient days, heraldic colours were specially chosen for their meaning; it almost became a form of alchemy. My earliest teacher in heraldry and lettering told me to mix 'metals with colours': in other words silver (white) with green was good but silver with gold (yellow) was bad. Makes sense doesn't it? Each colour means different things, however, in different countries. In Europe, black is the colour of death yet in the Orient it is often white, and so on. The meaning of colours may seem to be subjective in many cases but bear them in mind, nevertheless.

The Print and Production Manual
Practical Kit
BLUEPRINT

Below I have shown how some colours match others, as you can see some work some do not. Try and get hold of a colour wheel or, better still, a colour monitor and spend several hours seeing instantly what goes with what. The joy of DTP is that you can change colours and hues instantly so adjusting is easy, when you are happy you just press the button and out come your separations or, if you can afford it, out come your colour proofs.

It is worth while purchasing a good colour reference book showing the various hues and tones. Mine is in constant use.

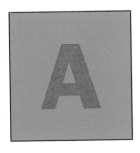  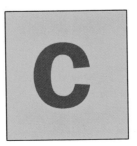 

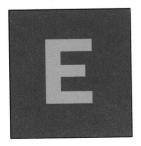  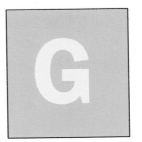 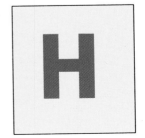

We should now look at how various colours look when matched with others. Firstly, colours on black. It is a great temptation to show colours out of a black background, it looks so strong and graphic. However, we should be aware of how these colours are used. If just for headline, then fine, go mad, but reds,greens and purples are not very pleasant to read in small type sizes. Blues, though attractive, are still hard to read, so try yellows, oranges and browns, even greys and you will see how nice they look.

White is, of course a fine background, but not for yellow. You would be surprised at the number of designers who will insist on printing yellow on white. Otherwise try colours of any type and enjoy the lift they give a page of type. It's also fun to try shadowing type for headlines against a colour, it gives the effect of three colours being used, spot colour, black and white. In fact tints of colours can give a spot-colour job an enormous increase in possibilities.

Colour monitors for computers have been available for several years and you can have some dazzling screens, showing anything you want. They are expensive but worth the extra money, just to see the effects of designs.

But, colour laser printers can be expensive, especially if you want high quality. The thermal wax printer provides good quality for proofing purposes at a reasonable cost. This prints on a special, smooth paper.

Notice how the different backgrounds affect the lettering, this is where the colour screen is vital. Try experimenting with various combinations.

Lorem ipsum dolor sit amet, consectetuer adipis

cing elit, sed diam non- ummy nibh euismod

tincidunt ut laoreet dolore magna aliquam

erat volutpat. Ut wisi enim ad minim veniam,

quis nostrud exerci tation ullamcorper suscipit

lobortis nisl ut aliquip ex ea commodo consequat.

Duis autem vel eum ir- iure dolor in hendrerit

in vulputate velit esse molestie consequat, vel

eu feugiat nulla facilisis at vero eros et accumsa

iusto odio dignissim qui blandit praesent luptatu

zzril delenit augue duis dolore te feugait nulla f

For the average DTP designer the capability of colour separation in DTP software can be used to produce separate pages for each colour. Some systems allow the designer to scan in colour art work, change it and produce colour proofs on the thermal printer but usually designers produce black and white separations to be given to a printing company to print in colour.

Colour should not be over-used. It is very tempting to make every element a separate colour but all this does is confuse the eye. Instead, think of what element you want to bring out or emphasise and just select that part. Too much does more harm than good.

Black

This is how the DTP system prints separations. Each sheet is a colour or tint and combined they make up the final printed job.
Each sheet or separation can be run out as film on an imagesetter, thus saving even more money.

Cyan

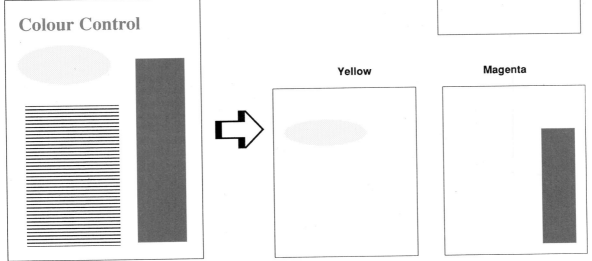

Yellow

Magenta

Your page make-up program should allow you to choose any colour in the spectrum simply by calling up menus and either naming the colour and letting the system do it for you or by defining the colour yourself. You select the text or image then apply the appropriate colour. If you use a monochrome monitor you can still apply colour but you will only see black and white or shades of grey.

A typical screen menu allows you to choose from the basic colours as shown below. If you wish to create a new one or a tint of one then you enter another menu

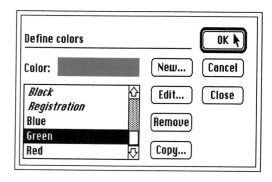

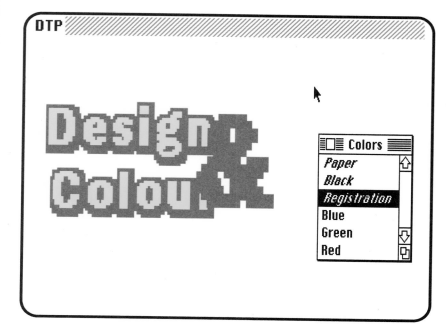

Here is another colour defining menu, this time it stays on screen so you don't have to go in and out of menus when you want to apply another colour. Think of each sheet of a separated job as transparent, so when you stick one on top of the other you would get the final effect. 'Registration marks' allow the printer to place the overlays in exactly the right position. If your page takes up the whole printing area then you can place the marks anywhere in the design and tell the printer to remove them when his positioning is complete

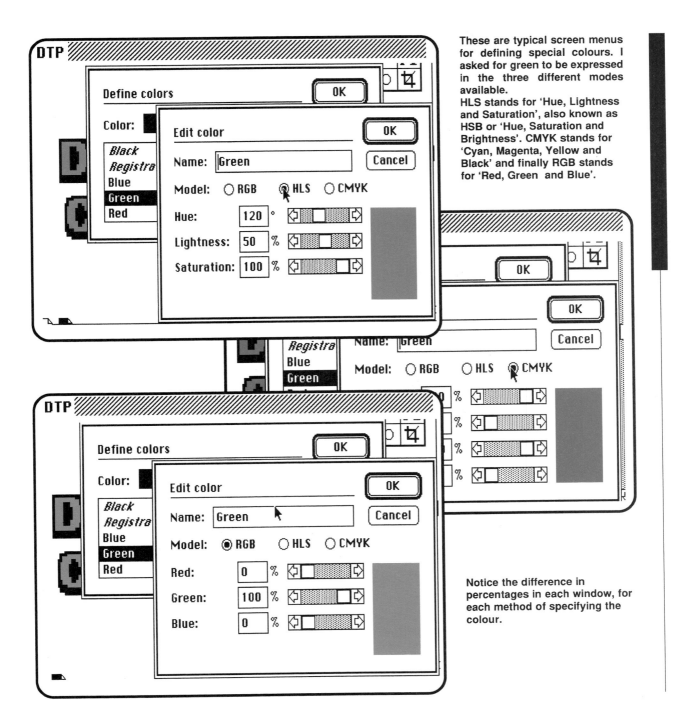

These are typical screen menus for defining special colours. I asked for green to be expressed in the three different modes available.

HLS stands for 'Hue, Lightness and Saturation', also known as HSB or 'Hue, Saturation and Brightness'. CMYK stands for 'Cyan, Magenta, Yellow and Black' and finally RGB stands for 'Red, Green and Blue'.

Notice the difference in percentages in each window, for each method of specifying the colour.

53

DTP is not just a new way of working and creating documents, it requires learning a whole new set of skills. Skills which previously we left to experts in those particular fields are now firmly back on our own doorstep and our responsibility. We have already looked at how typesetting has become part of a designer's life, resulting in the death of virtually all traditional setting shops. Well, I predict the same thing is going to happen with repro in the '90s. More of that in a later chapter. First let us understand how important colour skills are and how some of the basic ones work.

Specifying colour

We live in a Red, Green and Blue world – light being made up of Newton's spectrum of ROYGBIV. This is called natural light. We see it all around us and, with a peculiarity of the eye, we cannot filter it out. The eye is part of the brain, not an independent organ like the ear, and unlike the ear, which can filter out extraneous sounds, the eye takes in all colours, including those in the peripheral vision. As a result, colour must always be created with background in mind. Usually the white page. One other point worth mentioning here is the fact that one in ten males has some form of colour blindness. So some of the wonderful mixes of tones in your work could be completely missed by 10% of your male audience.

Printers' colours are another form available; they can create colours, such as 'Dayglo', which are unknown in the natural world. Lastly, we have projected colour, which is what we see on our screens.

Our colour monitors can work in monochrome, greyscale or RGB mode and will display a variety of shades and tints. How? Well, this is when it gets complex! The monitor screen is made up of pixels (or bits), the most basic description being two-bit. This gives just black and white, on or off. If you add more information to the pixel, you can get a greyscale – up to 256 steps, with 0 being solid hue and 255 pure white. Pixels can hold 8, 16, 24 or 32 bits of colour information but the higher the bit number, the greater the memory and processing power required to run the application. Several programs needs 32-bit colour to work properly and therefore need very powerful machines to drive them. Colour doesn't come cheap.

This RGB monitor is no help, however, when it comes to the world of repro. Cyan, magenta and yellow then become the order of the day. If we tried to print in RGB we would get 'black' by overprinting all three colours and the result is a dirty grey which is very blurred. To get crisp type and clean dark shadows we must add solid black or Keyline (K) to cyan, magenta and yellow to get CMYK. These are the colours that the printer uses and we should be specifying in them. All these pretty Pantones we ask for are a nightmare to the average printer, so it is far better to get a tint book from him and look up the mix you want and specify as such.

Having said that, let's get back to our monitor merrily showing colours in RGB. If you are working correctly and making up your palette in CMYK, the computer has to use a simple formula to change the colours to RGB so that it can display them on screen. This CLUT or Colour Look-Up Table is not 100% accurate and neither is the screen, so NEVER MAKE COLOUR DECISIONS USING SCREEN RESOLUTIONS. (Every monitor needs re-calibrating or colour adjusting, preferably every day. Many quality monitors have calibrators which attach to the screen and self-calibrate. If yours doesn't then at least call up a basic palette and compare it with your printer's tint book. You will see the difference!) So define your colour in CMYK by looking it up in a tint book. The output will then be exactly the percentage you want even if it doesn't look like it on screen.

There are, however, new developments in colour specifying which should be mentioned here. Firstly, the CIE, or Commission Internationale de l'Eclairage which is a body set up to specify colour, using scientific definition rather than subjective methods which can be affected by ambient light and personal observation. Basically, a Belgian pink will be exactly the same as a Taihitian pink. Secondly, an exciting method of specifying colour in the publishing and graphics world is Focoltone. Similar to other colour models in style and content, it uses only the printer's world of CMYK. The swatches are exceptional in quality and range, yet all are achievable with a four-colour mix, not a fifth colour in sight.

REVERSALS

The long valued technique of reversing type or images out of a colour or plain black is simplicity itself on a DTP system. In general black text on white is the most legible way of presenting the written word. White out of black (WOB), however, looks great, if used sparingly, but can be virtually unreadable. Depending on the standard of the final printing the reversed text can almost disappear because our eyes get upset when reading large amounts of reversed-out type, as anyone who spends a long time on a standard computer screen will tell you. The same applies with black on tint/tone (BOT) as you saw in the previous section on tints.

This problem is magnified when type is reversed-out of four-colours and there is imperfect registration. Look at any magazine or newspaper and you may see typical examples of this problem. It is even more apparent when using a serif face or a face in a small size, because the finer lines will fill in.

Sometimes the design calls for reversed type and these points must be borne in mind. Heavier faces such as Bookman and Franklin, which have less difference between thickness of stems and arms, are best suited for reversing. Consider using bold or larger sizes in finer faces, but they may need extra leading and spacing to counter their up and down effect.

Lorem ipsum dolor sit amet, consectetuer adipiscing elit, sed diam nonummy nibh euismod tincidunt ut laoreet dolore magna aliquam erat volutpat. Ut wisi enim ad minim veniam, quis nostrud exerci tation ullamcorper suscipit lobortis nisl ut aliquip ex ea commodo consequat. Duis autem vel eum iriure dolor in hendrerit in vulputate velit esse molestie consequat, vel illum dolore eu feugiat nulla

Above was set in 8 point Times and, as you can see totally illegible. This is better, it's Helvetica 10 point bold. Lobortis nisl ut aliquip ex ea commodo consequat. Duis autem vel eum iriure dolor in hendrerit in vulputate velit esse molestie consequat, vel illum dolore

Quia uis magnast ipsus, et alte aera per purum grauter simulcra ferunter, et feriunt oculus turbantia compositus. Preatera splendor quicumque est acer adurit saepa oculus, ideo quod semina. Urida preatera fiunt tuentur arqutrie quia luroris

De compore eonum semina multa fluent simulcris. Quia uis magnast ipsus, et alte aera per purum grauter simulcra ferunter, et feriunt oculus turbantia compositus. Preatera splendor quicumque est acer adurit saepa

Two examples of text that has been reversed as white out of black (WOB). Both are in 12 point, the top one is Times, a serif face and below is Helvetica a sans serif. Note the way the serifs are affected.

Text wraps and flows

This used to be another laborious job before the advent of DTP as any image or cut-out used with text running closely round the shape had to be cast-off carefully. A cut-out is a picture that has an irregular edge or border. They can be very effective in a page of text especially if the type surrounds it well, one gets a feeling of an island of image in a sea of words, a very pleasant graphic effect. But how do we do it?

First, choose the right sort of image — one with a pleasing shape when cut out. Place on the page, in position, and either scan and place or use tracing paper. This technique means the tracing of the image on fine tracing paper and then taping in position over the DTP screen and drawing round the outline with the cursor. Crude but effective! The page can then be run out and the original image can be pasted in by the printer.

Text can now be run round the outline either by hand or automatically, depending on the make-up system you use. Most programs will allow you to position a shape on the page and will wrap the text around it almost instantly. The savings in time and money makes this technique perfect for DTP usage. Another big problem in some of the cruder make-up programs is hyphenation. If this is not very good you can end up with those wonderfully named "Widows and Orphans". These are single words or worse still, parts of words, that are left hanging in a line all on their own at the end of a paragraph. These will then have to be altered by hand, usually by editing out a word or two on screen. This is a vital job as they are most unsightly.

Lorem ipsum dolor sit amet, consectetuer adipiscing elit, sed diam nonummy nibh euismod tincidunt ut laoreet dolore magna aliquam erat volutpat. Ut wisi enim ad minim veniam, quis nostrud exerci tation ullamcorper suscipit lobortis nisl ut aliquip ex ea commodo consequat. Duis autem vel eum iriure dolor in hendrerit in vulputate velit esse molestie consequat, vel illum dolore.

Eu feugiat nulla nest i

This is an orphan

facilisis.
vero eros et accumsan et iusto odio dignissim qui blandit praesent luptatum zzril delenit augue duis dolore te feugait nulla facilisi. Lorem ipsum dolor sit amet, consectetuer adipiscing elit, sed diam nonummy nibh euismod tincidunt ut laoreet dolore magna aliquam erat volutpat. Ut wisi enim ad minim veniam, quis nostrud exerci tation ullamcorper suscipit lobortis nisl ut al-

This is a widow

✔ KEY POINTS

- The reader's eye must not become lost
- There are no hard and fast rules — only guidelines

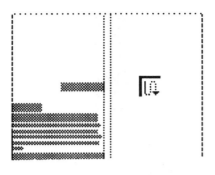

TEXT FLOWS

When compiling a long document a perennial problem facing the designer is the inevitable changes that the client makes after the pages are made up. For example, if the face has to be changed or the leading throughout needs

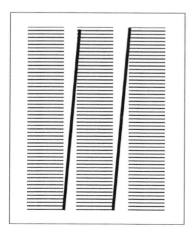

Text flow

When compiling a long document a perennial problem facing the designer is the inevitable changes that the client makes after the pages are made up. For example, if the face has to be changed or the leading throughout needs more space and so on, it can be done very simply on most modern DTP systems, without having to work through it page by page.

The same applies when text must flow from page to page on a long document. If a picture has to be fitted in or more text must be inserted, it can be done on screen and the text will flow from the new insertion point on to the next page and so on. A huge improvement to the old nightmare of re-pasting a whole set of art work.

Headers, footers and folios

These are important devices for long documents, magazines, books or papers that keep the reader informed. They enable them to monitor their progress through the document. Running heads or headers are, as their name implies, the top line heading, usually in the margin, denoting the section or chapter title. These can be inserted in the grid make-up stage and pose no real problem except choice of face. Often an italicised face is used.

The same applies with running feet or footers which are the same information set at the bottom margin of a page. This information probably will include the 'folio' or page numbers. These folios can look striking when enclosed in a box or strap — I have used this style on the book grid throughout.

✔ KEYPOINTS

Help the readers know where they are in the document

Use automatic facilities to layout lengthy runs of copy

HEADERS

HEADERS

HEADERS

HEADERS

HEADERS

HEADERS

HEADERS

HEADERS

HEADERS

Left are some headers you could use or adapt, the possiblities are vast.

17

21

12

10

Here are some ideas for folios or page numbers, you must be able to think of dozens more.

126

②

DTP in Action

HOUSE STYLE

Every company or organisation has a unique trademark or logo which is the recognisable motif of their 'house'. It really is a form of chivalric emblem, no different from the banners and shields of Medieval times. These were a swift identifying mark that could be easily recognised and so it is today with a house style. This means a generic design style that can be applied in a variety of ways to an organisation's literature from business cards to advertisements. It should encompass everything from typeface to choice of colour, and once decided upon should be rigorously adhered to. There is no point in a company spending a small fortune designing a house style that three months later they alter and discard, so make sure you have everyone's approval before applying the design to all the company's products and literature. Again this is where DTP comes into its own;changes or 'tweaking' can be achieved with the minimum of time and effort. But be careful; here also lies the biggest drawback of the DTP phenomena — *the client changeability factor.*

What happens is the client finds out how simple it is to change a design on DTP as opposed to the conventional method so he or she begins to jiggle things around, almost for the sake of it. I think its unintentional but the rules are:

• Keep the client away from the set up, certainly when you are working on their job. It's fatal for them to sit and watch you change things with such ease.

• Be firm. Don't put up with too much alteration, what happens then is that the design becomes more and more diluted. Help them to come to a decision and then keep them to it — if possible!

LOGOS

A logo is like a hallmark, it identifies a product or organisation and differentiates it from other similar companies. As such it is a valuable commodity and the design must be considered in this light. The logo can be a simple graphic device, a complex lettering symbol or just the company's name in a unique typeface.

Firstly, try to make the logo non-specific as far as period is

If we try to make a logo for QT Ltd using their initials you can see the difference position makes...

...here it reads TQ. The repositioning is so simple with DTP, use 'send to back' and 'bring to front' commands.

This one could be either TQ or QT. Ambiguous positioning is bad design in logo creation, the name or motif must be clear.

Swift changes on screen make fast new ideas practical, it's scribbling really in a note form. Sooner or later you will find the position or style that meets the brief.

These quick alternatives, by 'copy and paste,' were done in minutes instead of painstakingly tracing or drawing the letters each time. There are dozens of ways of treating just simple initials.

You can design a face of your own using the drawing tools available on most DTP systems.

✔ KEYPOINTS

Lettering logos must be legible

Logos must be immediately recognisable even when they are abstract

They must be adaptable - in size and colour

Use the "send to back" command to place elements

Let us use an imaginary restaurant called 'Rendezvous' as an example of a typestyle logo. First see how the various type faces give a different impression. Begin by just typing the word.

Rendezvous

That's fine as a straight forward face but the place is a romantic French restaurant.

Rendezvous

Unless the place was a trendy rock place this is too heavyweight.

Rendezvous

This Zapf Chancery is a little too sugary for my taste in this context.

Rendezvous

This is Palatino, not bad but a bit 'dry' for a logo

Rendezvous

Ah — that's it. Seville has the right combination of weight and romance. How about if I...

Rendezvous

Great — even the client likes it!

concerned. Fashion is a fickle mistress and the hip logo of today is the boring, quaint, old trademark of tomorrow. The best trademarks and logos are undatable.

Secondly, discover which market your client is in, or aiming for — there is no point in making a welding company look dainty. Analyse the market and zero in on it by creating the design to communicate instantly to that niche.

Thirdly, allow a lot of room for manoeuvre in the sizing and manipulation of the logo. Remember, the client may want it 3mm deep on a business card and up to 6 metres high for a banner, so keep it flexible.

Type style logo. A lot of companies just want their name as the logo, but this doesn't mean that you can't use lots of design sense in a logo.

The device could be a stylised signature or a unique typeface that reflects the organisation's stance or marketplace. Choose a face that reflects their style and approach. Otherwise, a motif can be made up from the name itself, making it a design of its own, neither image nor text. Keep in mind that we are in the business of communication — keep it legible.

Allusive logo . Also called associate logos, these logos are a graphic device that pictorially represents the company's stance or product, without necessarily using words. They are often a sort of visual pun or abstract hallmark that identifies the product instantly, a picture tells a thousand words, or purely decorative. See if you can distil the organisation's essence into a few lines.

Rendezvous

Rendezvous

Now, thanks to copy, cut and paste, you can play around with positions as much as you or the client likes until you are happy. Here the house style is ranged left and right...

Rendezvous

...and even dropped into the centre like this. Quite effective although impractical. Break the rules! Be different! The wonder of DTP is the ease of change. These all took minutes to produce and print out an almost finished sheet.

LETTERHEADS

Until recently, letterheads were staid and dull, just writing paper with the organisation's address. Now, however, company stationery is an extension of marketing, to the outside world, showing all the flair and style of an advertisement.

When considering a house style, find out who you are aiming at and what image you are hoping to create.

OK Tee Shirts Inc.
Hallway Drive
Coland 833726
(0998) 967754

If you want an image or tint to bleed off the page make sure that you allow extra area off the crop marks to allow for the cutter missing by a few millimetres.

351 Antrobus Street, Yorkdale, Farley B89 Y77

Remember to use logos or graphics to liven up a corporate identity, no matter how humble.

Let's take as another example: a coach company called

AUTOBUS

There is no point in setting it in

AUTOBUS

They want a tough, modern image, this is too light...

AUTOBUS

...so let us try Franklin

AUTOBUS

Better but dull, we need movement so...

AUTOBUS

Do you see how easy it is to change feel and style with just a few keystrokes? Now to fine tune...

AUTOBUS

Finally we come up with this one.

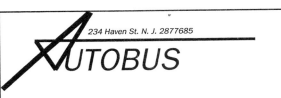

234 Haven St. N. J. 2877685

SCHEDULE

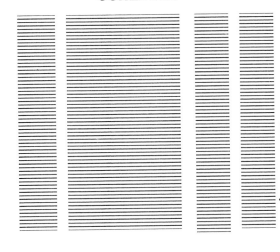

234 Haven St. N. J. 2877685

WITH COMPLIMENTS

**From this logo we can develop
letterheads, invoices, cards and so on**

234 Haven St. N. J. 2877685

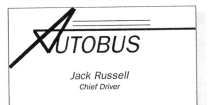

Jack Russell
Chief Driver

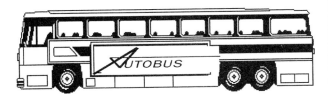

A.J. Joseph Inc.
CONSTRUCTION

——— o ———

Invoice Number _____   Date _____

Details	Cost

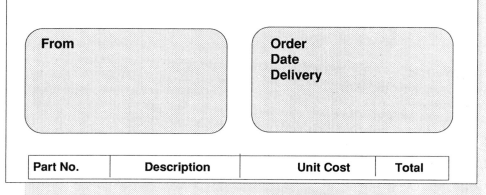

A.J. JOSEPH INC.
CONSTRUCTION

From

Order
Date
Delivery

Part No.	Description	Unit Cost	Total

A form may be easier to read or fill in if the parts that need completion are tinted or coloured

FORMS, INVOICES AND QUESTIONNAIRES

A major part of the DTP designer's life is spent doing the mundane task of making bureaucracy palatable. This is seldom more apparent than when designing forms, invoices and questionnaires. Any kind of document that requires completion can be daunting (Tax returns) or pleasant (Christmas list), it depends on the purpose and the layout. Now we can't do anything about the former but we can certainly help with the latter.

The first consideration is what information is required? How can it be obtained? How is it to be retrieved and used? In an invoice or statement this is pretty obvious, all we want to show is how much a customer owes, from when, to whom and for what. Don't forget to show any local taxes due, registered numbers and credit arrangements, if any. If the client is using what is known as a NCR (No Carbon Required) set of self-duplicating forms, you may be required to rigidly keep to a specific format. This is often because the computer that retrieves the information must have the information laid out in precise positions, so keep to them.

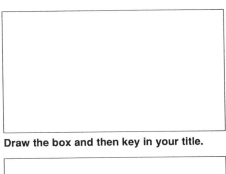

Draw the box and then key in your title.

Delivery Address:

Aligning boxes and pieces of copy is essential in form design, without this, the design looks a mess. Keep to one typeface — peferably one that matches the house style.

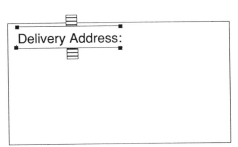

Delivery Address:

Shift the title around in the boxes, this is sometimes easier in a drawing program.

Delivery Address:

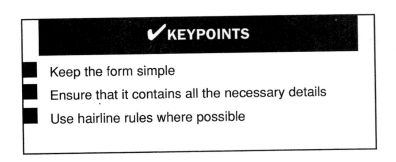

Questionnaires

Questionnaires can be a simple 'Tick here...' type or require detailed written replies or even a combination of both. Most marketing companies or data capture companies like tick boxes because the operators who retrieve the answers to the questions just put 'Yes' or 'No' to a series of numbered boxes. These are keyed into the computer as data and can be manipulated in various ways, but the trickiest part is making the interviewee *want* to answer in the first place.

Making these forms less daunting is a difficult task. To a certain extent they should be fun to fill in, so try to design around an easy-to-follow, logical pattern. Try not to cram too many questions on one side or page, that will frighten the reader. Instead give the form space to breathe, allow the reader to feel there is lots of time to complete the form.

Finally, if you are asking the reader to answer with an opinion or fuller reply, don't give them half a line on which to write, especially when you say in brackets (No more than 50 words please). Give them several lines, lots of space and they will open up more.

21. How did you evaluate the service?

☐ Very good
☐ Good
☐ Fair
☐ Poor
☐ Appalling

This is good standard style for the tick box type of quesionnaire, question in bold with number prominent. Easy to answer.

22. At which other hotels have you stayed?

_____

_____

This is the trickier question, it has not got a 'yes' or 'no' answer, so allow generous space for the reply or the interviewee just will not answer. It is no good doing this...

23. Give your overall impression of your stay?
(please give details)

_____

24. And so on...

See what I mean?

How old are you?

Under 12	☐
13	☐
14	☐
15	☐
16	☐
17	☐
18	☐
19	☐
Over 19	☐

How many of these type of games do you own?

	1-3	4-6	7-9	10+
Simulation Games	☐	☐	☐	☐
Arcade Games	☐	☐	☐	☐
Strategy Games	☐	☐	☐	☐
Adventure Games	☐	☐	☐	☐
War Games	☐	☐	☐	☐
Shoot-'em-ups	☐	☐	☐	☐

How many of the following types of games do you buy each month?

	1-3	4-6	7-9	10+
Budget Games	☐	☐	☐	☐
Full Priced Games	☐	☐	☐	☐

How many people have read or looked at this copy of Sinclair User?

None	☐
1	☐
2	☐
3	☐
4	☐
More	☐

Which of these other computer magazines do you read regularly?(i.e. at least one out of every two issues)

Computer & Video Games	☐
Computer Gamer	☐
Popular Computing Weekly	☐
Your Sinclair	☐
Sinclair User	☐
Crash	☐
Your Computer	☐

PLEASE ANSWER THE FOLLOWING QUESTIONS:

A What is your job title?
Please tick one of the following:

1	☐	Chairman
2	☐	Partner
3	☐	Chief Executive
4	☐	Managing Director

Or tick one title from List 1 and a job function from List 2:

List 1

5	☐	Director
8	☐	Executive
6	☐	Manager

List 2

9	☐	DP/MIS
7	☐	Sales
10	☐	Marketing
11	☐	Training
12	☐	Technical
13	☐	Production
14	☐	Finance

B Which of the following best describes your main business, organisation or industry?

1	☐	Accounting
3	☐	Advertising
6	☐	Architectural &Construction
8	☐	The Arts
17	☐	Computer Industry
23	☐	Education
25	☐	Energy
11	☐	Finance & Insurance
15	☐	Government & Civil Service
32	☐	Health Services
36	☐	Legal Services
37	☐	Leisure
38	☐	Management Consultancy
39	☐	Manufacturing
27	☐	Media & Communications
42	☐	Print Supplies & Services
44	☐	Public Services
43	☐	Publicity & PR
45	☐	Publishing
51	☐	Research & Development
52	☐	Retail & Service
16	☐	Technical Consultancy
47	☐	Telecommunications
9	☐	Trade & Professional Bodies

A classic standby like this still grabs the attention, regardless how corny. Something for nothing.

Reversals can help in a cheap budget job: they draw attention to the headline. Just key in the text, draw the reversed shape and send it to the back. Then highlight the text and reverse it.

PAMPHLETS, FLYERS AND TICKETS

These humble design jobs are often the 'below the line' work that you will find on your desk from many of your clients, but a good designer can turn these bread-and-butter briefs into solid stuff by using the DTP system wisely. Don't treat them as throw-aways or you will treat the design the same way. Put the same amount of skill into anything you do, it's a discipline that won't let you down.

Pamphlets can be four-colour flashy inserts, mailshots or simple street give-aways. If they have lots of illustrations showing products, try wraparounds. They are very effective and hold interest sometimes more than the regimented stamp album approach. You will often find that there is a lot of copy to be fitted in this type of work, so bear in mind the rules of type size and line length.

The main role of pamphlets and flyers is information, either getting people to realise the availability of some thing or some service. Communication is vital because you only have a brief second for the reader to glance at the design and decide whether to throw it away, read it and then dispose of it or read it and keep it.

✔ KEYPOINTS

Do not treat flyers and pamphlets as throw-aways

Grab the reader's attention — then keep it

WIN

First the grabber... but win what?

Now introduce a picture, either scanned or dropped in by the printer showing the prize or the product. This is the part where you intensify the reader's interest — 'keep me' screams the flyer.

'Win this house?' ask the readers; they must know more! So they read on. Here you qualify the grabber with details and prompt the reader to 'do' something. This is the basic approach, obviously the idea would be far more subtle than this.

Find a simple headline or good image to get the attention of readers and then consolidate with solid design techniques. You should find some examples that have caught your eye and find out why; then adapt them for yourself. It isn't copying — there is nothing new under the sun, so all you are doing is adapting existing ideas the same as we all have done.

WIN

This dream house could be yours if you scoot along with this to Jason's Estate Offices today!
The new estate at Barton Mills is just where you would like to live so why not buy and try these beautiful executive houses. Ring 0998-86878

Tickets

Tickets play an important role; they carry information about the event, such as times and places, therefore keep them clear and concise. Don't forget you may need to give seating details such as row and seat number. Does it need a perforation for a tear-off stub? Does it need security numbering?

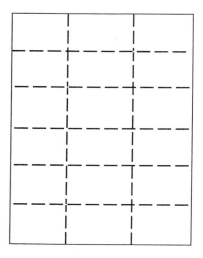

F:60447

J 17

Patrons are requested not to smoke in the auditorium. Interval drinks may be reserved at the bar before the performance

The way to create small items on a DTP page is to divide it up like this. Make up one ticket in a box and copy and paste it in all the others. Then print on thicker paper and cut them up. Don't try this process if you have 60,000 to run off — give it to a printer. This same procedure can be used with business cards and the like.

New Releases

Lorem ipsum dolor sit amet, consectetuer adipiscing elit, sed diam nonummy nibh euismod tincidunt ut laoreet dolore magna aliquam erat volutpat. Ut wisi enim ad minim veniam, quis nostrud exerci tation ullamcorper suscipit lobortis nisl ut aliquip ex ea commodo consequat. Duis autem vel eum iriure dolor in hendrerit in vulputate velit esse molestie consequat, vel illum dolore eu feugait nulla facilisis at vero eros et accumsan et iusto odio dignissim qui blandit praesent luptatum zzril delenit augue duis dolore te feugait nulla facilisi.

Dolor sit amet consectetuer adipiscing elit, sed diam nonummy nibh euismod tincidunt ut laoreet dolore magna aliquam erat volutpat. Ut wisi enim ad minim veniam, quis nostrud exerci tation ullamcorper sus-

cipit lobortis nisl ut aliquip ex ea commodo consequat.

Duis autem vel eum iriure dolor in hendrerit in vulputate velit esse molestie consequat, vel illum dolore eu feugiat nulla facilisis at vero eros et accumsan et iusto odio dignissim qui blandit praesent luptatum zzril delenit augue duis dolore te feugait nulla facilisi. Nam liber tempor cum soluta nobis eleifend option congue nihil imperdiet doming id quod mazim placerat facer possim assum. Lorem ipsum dolor sit amet,

Consectetuer adipiscing elit, sed diam nonummy nibh euismod tincidunt ut laoreet dolore magna aliquam erat volutpat. Ut wisi enim ad minim veniam, quis nostrud exerci tation ullamcorper suscipit lobortis nisl ut aliquip ex ea commodo consequat. Duis autem vel eum iriure dolor in hendrerit in vulputate velit esse molestie consequat, vel illum dolore eu feugiat nulla facilisis at vero

eros et accumsan et iusto odio dignissim qui blandit praesent luptatum zzril delenit augue duis dolore te feugait nulla facilisi. Lorem ipsum dolor sit amet, consectetuer adipiscing elit, sed diam nonummy nibh euismod tincidunt ut laoreet dolore magna aliquam erat volutpat.

Ut wisi enim ad minim veniam, quis nostrud exerci tation ullamcorper suscipit lobortis nisl ut aliquip ex ea commodo consequat. Duis autem vel eum iriure dolor in hendrerit in vulputate velit esse molestie consequat, vel eros et accumsan et iusto odio dignissim qui blandit praesent luptatum zzril delenit augue duis dolore te feugait nulla facilisi. Lorem ipsum dolor sit amet, consectetuer adipiscing elit, sed diam nonummy nibh euismod tincidunt ut laoreet dolore magna aliquam erat volutpat. Ut wisi enim ad minim veniam, quis nostrud exerci tation ullamcorper suscipit

lobortis nisl ut aliquip ex ea commodo consequat. Duis autem vel eum iriure dolor in hendrerit in vulputate velit esse molestie consequat, vel illum dolore eu feugiat nulla facilisis at vero eros et accumsan et iusto odio dignissim qui blandit praesent luptatum zzril delenit augue duis dolore te feugait nulla facilisi.

Lorem ipsum dolor sit amet, consectetuer adipiscing elit, sed diam nonummy nibh euismod tincidunt ut laoreet dolore magna aliquam erat volutpat. Ut wisi enim ad minim veniam, quis nostrud exerci tation ullamcorper suscipit lobortis nisl ut aliquip ex ea commodo consequat. Duis autem vel eum iriure dolor in hendrerit in vulputate velit esse molestie consequat, vel illum dolore eu feugiat nulla facilisis at vero eros et accumsan et iusto odio dignissim qui blandit praesent luptatum zzril de-

CATALOGUES AND PRICE LISTS

Listing a lot of information attractively requires typographical skill and design flair. Catalogues usually require a number of objects laying out in cramped space with copy. This can be helped by grouping pictures. You often have to make do with handout PR photos to work on as there is neither the time nor the budget to take directed shots. Try wraparounds again, they don't use up much space and can be very impressive. With modern DTP techniques this method is not as daunting as it used to be.

Careful use of rules can also give the crowded page a sense of order. The readers of catalogues are browsers; they are usually 'sold' on the product already, so what you are really offering is a sort of menu. Therefore the sales pitch does not need to be as hard hitting as a flyer.

With lists of any kind you must beware of confusing the eye with too much information in tabulated form. Either shorten the line length or use bands of tone, rules and so on, to help the eye to move along the line easily. It is very frustrating to get half way along a line of information and lose your position and have to start again. If your reader needs to use their finger or a ruler to read the list, you are not doing your job!

The bottom two examples show a typical catalogue laid out using DTP techniques. On the left I've used no pictures but typographically broken up the text with thin rules between columns and bold headlines. On the right, the pictures have been dropped in using wrap around and trimmed closely manually. The effect, I think you will agree, is far more satisfactory. Always use pictures when possible.

New Releases

Lorem ipsum dolor sit amet, consectetuer adipiscing elit, sed diam nonummy nibh euismod tincidunt ut laoreet dolore magna aliquam erat volutpat. Ut wisi enim ad minim veniam, quis nostrud exerci tation ullamcorper suscipit lobortis nisl ut aliquip ex ea commodo consequat. Duis autem vel eum iriure dolor in hendrerit in vulputate velit esse molestie consequat, vel illum dolore eu feugiat nulla facilisis at vero eros et accumsan et iusto odio dignissim qui blandit praesent luptatum zzril delenit augue duis dolore te feugait nulla facilisi.

Dolor sit amet consectetuer adipiscing

elit, sed diam nonummy nibh euismod tincidunt ut laoreet dolore magna aliquam erat volutpat. Ut wisi enim ad minim veniam, quis nostrud exerci tation ullamcorper suscipit lobortis nisl ut aliquip ex ea commodo consequat.

Duis autem vel eum iriure dolor in hendrerit in vulputate velit esse molestie consequat, vel illum dolore eu feugiat nulla facilisis at vero eros et accumsan et iusto odio dignissim qui blandit praesent luptatum zzril delenit augue duis dolore te feugait nulla facilisi. Nam liber tempor cum soluta nobis eleifend option congue nihil iin vulputate velit esse molestiemperdiet doming id quod mazim placerat facer possim assum. Lorem ipsum dolor sit amet, in vulputate velit esse molestie

Consectetuer adipiscing elit, sed diam nonummy nibh euismod tincidunt ut laoreet dolore magna aliquam erat volutpat. Ut wisi enim ad minim veniam, quis nostrud exerci tation ullamcorper suscipit lobortis nisl ut aliquip ex ea commodo consequat. Duis autem vel eum iriure dolor in hendrerit in vulputate velit esse molestie consequat, vel illum dolore eu feugiat nulla facilisis at vero eros et accumsan et iusto odio dignissim qui blandit praesent luptatum zzril delenit augue duis dolore te feugait nulla facilisi. Lorem ipsum dolor sit amet, consectetuer adipiscing elit, sed diam nonummy nibh euismod tincidunt ut laoreet dolore magna aliquam erat volutpat.

Ut wisi enim ad minim veniam, quis nostrud

exerci tation ullamcorper suscipit lobortis nisl ut aliquip ex ea commodo consequat. Duis autem vel eum iriure dolor in hendrerit in vulputate velit esse molestie consequat, vel illum dolore eu feugiat nulla facilisis at vero eros et accumsan et iusto odio dignissim qui blandit praesent luptatum zzril delenit augue duis dolore te feugait nulla facilisi. Lorem ipsum dolor sit amet, consectetuer adipiscing elit, sed diam nonummy nibh euismod tincidunt ut laoreet dolore magna aliquam erat volutpat. Ut wisi enim ad minim veniam, quis nostrud exerci tation ullamcorper suscipit lobortis nisl ut aliquip ex ea commodo consequat. Duis autem vel eum iriure dolor in hendrerit in vulputate velit esse molestie consequat, vel illum dolore eu feugiat nulla facilisis at vero eros et

ADVERTISEMENTS

These come in various categories, from the small advert in the local newspaper to the flashy big display in a glossy magazine. All advertisements follow these basic rules.
They must:

- **Inform**
- **Create desire**
- **Invite response**

Also, all products and services must have a Unique Selling Point (USP) — this is why they are in the market place; they are different or better or cheaper than the rest. Find out this USP and sell it like mad.

Let us take a hypothetical company by the name of 'Global' and look at selling its products through advertisements. First I have designed a logo using a drawing package.

But 'Global' could produce anything, it could be, and probably is, a travel company. However, we have not stressed the Unique Selling Point (USP).

So we add the USP — in this case an astonishing one — and then the angle of the logo makes sense. Without the explanatory line underneath the logo was meaningless. Now we have a pseudo-rug trade mark and must think of a way of selling its products through the media.

The next task is to think of a snappy headline. This can be witty or straightforward, depending on the brief. In this case the client wants it to be light so I came up with —

Now here we see a design fault. Look at the exclamation mark , see how it almost matches the preceeding 'I'. This is confusing, which means bad communication. Therefore we can either add letter spacing to separate the 'I' and '!' or delete the '!' altogether. I opt for the latter as it is only an emphasis to the 'gag' in the headline.

Adding the body copy resolves the questions posed in the mind of the reader by the headline and clarifies what the advertisement is selling. The size and weight of the headline against the body copy are like speech. Think of the advert actually talking to the reader — it shouts 'We won't...' then says 'Think of the money...' in a normal conversational tone. If you bear this in mind it makes the designing of an advertisement far simpler. What is important is shouted (i.e. bigger) and then spoken and you can even whisper in small type sizes. You can be ironic with italics or treat an aside in brackets. The advert must 'talk' to the reader. This is not a very inspired piece of design but serves to crudely show how the various elements can be put together on the computer.

We won't take you for a ride — but our carpets will!

We won't take you for a ride —

but our carpets will

Think of the money you will save on travelling to and from work using our special Commuter Rug in formal grey or outrageous pink. Test drive one today!

TEKNIK

Hardly the engineering look the client wants.

For once you can be really creative, thinking up catchy headlines, witty images and snappy copy. You will probably have to do the lot! If not and you are supplied with copy and a rough layout then half the job is done for you, never forgetting that you, as the final designer, have a say in the overall advertisement as well. Every advertisement, be it a quarter page in a trade magazine or a whole page series in the national Press, is a chance for you to prove what a wizard you are on the DTP system.

Teknik

The face is better but it needs to tell a visual story, so...

Here, I have invented an engineering company called Teknik who manufacture a revolutionary new screw — the Z-Head. The logo needed to reflect the company's commitment to screws so I added that element to the logo. I also felt that it needed a 3-dimensional effect as the product was used to hold pieces of material together hence the dropped shadows.

✔ **KEYPOINTS**

- Discover the Unique Selling Point and emphasise that in the advertisement
- Make the type 'talk'
- Communicate!

Teknik

TFR/1

☐ Please send me details of your revolutionary new Z-Head screws
☐ Please send a representative to our offices

Name _____ Position _____

Company Name _____

Address _____

_____ Code _____

Teknik Screws Inc. Unit 123, Investment Industrial Estate, E.S. 127734

The client wants a reply coupon and basic details of action required by the prospect, so use tick boxes for yes/no answers. Either draw them or use a dingbat.

The form is small but need not be cramped. The prospect will have to fill in their name and address, so give them plenty of room. Also it is advisable to change type size by at least two points from the body copy in the advertisement.

This little device is a marketing ploy to see which advertisements pull the most response. This stands for the magazine — Technical Fastenings Review/First insertion. So any replies on this coupon can be monitored by the marketing people and the data is used to plan future campaigns.

WE USED OUR HEADS TO GET IT TOGETHER

orem ipsum dolor sit amet, consectetuer adipiscing elit, sed diam nonummy nibh euismod tincidunt ut laoreet dolore magna aliquam erat volutpat. Ut wisi enim ad minim veniam, quis nostrud exerci tation ullamcorper suscipit lobortis nisl ut aliquip ex ea commodo consequat. Duis autem vel eum iriure dolor in hendrerit in vulputate velit esse molestie consequat, vel illum dolore eu feugiat nulla facilisis at vero eros et accumsan et iusto odio dignissim qui blandit praesent luptatum zzril

This is a diagram of the Z-Head imported from a drawing package and now ready to be placed on the page.

This is the technical talk relating to the screw head, it explains how it works and why it works. Therefore it will be placed near the diagram. I have also set it in the same face as the headline.

The headline needed something witty but pertinent, perhaps this works. Anyway the client is delighted and now we must put all the elements together to make up the advertisement.

WE USED OUR HEADS TO GET IT TOGETHER

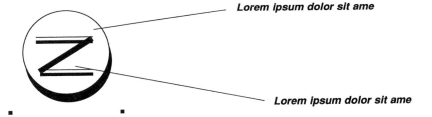

Lorem ipsum dolor sit ame

Lorem ipsum dolor sit ame

Lorem ipsum dolor sit amet, consectetuer adipiscing elit, sed diam nonummy nibh euismod tincidunt ut laoreet dolore magna aliquam erat volutpat. Ut wisi enim ad minim veniam, quis nostrud exerci tation ullamcorper suscipit lobortis nisl ut aliquip ex ea commodo consequat. Duis autem vel eum iriure dolor in hendrerit in vulputate velit esse molestie consequat, vel illum dolore eu feugiat nulla facilisis at vero eros et accumsan et iusto odio dignissim qui blandit praesent luptatum zzril

Lorem ipsum dolor sit amet, consectetuer adipiscing elit, sed diam nonummy nibh euismod tincidunt ut laoreet dolore magna aliquam erat volutpat. Ut wisi enim ad minim veniam, quis nostrud exerci tation ullamcorper suscipit lobortis nisl ut aliquip ex ea commodo consequat. Duis autem vel eum iriure dolor in hendrerit in vulputate velit

NEWSPAPERS AND MAGAZINES

Probably the first universally accepted use of DTP was in periodical publishing. So many periodicals are produced or semi-produced on computers now it is impossible to list them all. In the early days of DTP it was easy to recognise their style, a trifle amateurish. But now with so many typefaces and such typographical control it means that if you're not desktop publishing, you're lagging badly behind.

4	**1**
Back Cover	Front Cover

2	**3**
Inside Left	Inside Right

The flat plan is a plan of pages used in all publications whether it is a book or a house journal. Above is the simplest flat plan for a double sided single sheet journal. You can see when folded, how the document will fall.

You must use the company style as this will dictate the style of the journal. Use a typeface in keeping with general material produced for the company.

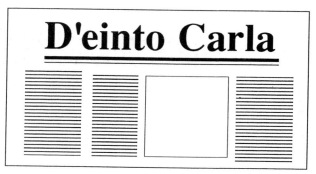

House journals are amongst the first things which DTP designers get to work on. It's the perfect method of producing a monthly, short run, limited circulation title with little outlay. The trouble is that often the job is given to someone from the typing pool in the hope that they can knock it up, usually with disastrous results. House journals are frequently sent to customers and suppliers of an organisation, as well as employees, and if the standard is poor it reflects badly. Therefore they should not be treated lightly but should be top quality journals. As usual, our first consideration is 'to whom are we communicating, and what are we showing them?' Find out your market and your client's image. Does the journal want to look classy or chummy. Is the client a firm of management consultants or a whoopee cushion manufacturer? Use the house style as a spring board and develop the magazine around that. Try to use photographs and help develop a sense of camaraderie within the organisation.

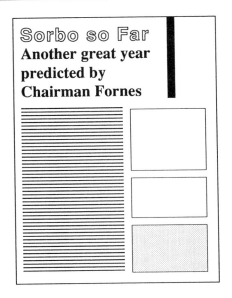

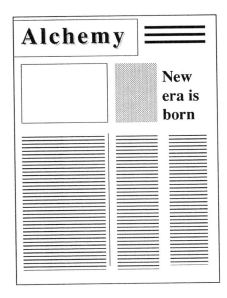

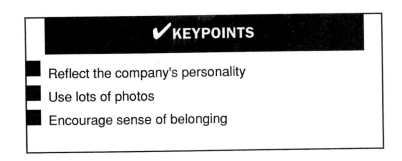

✔ KEYPOINTS

- Reflect the company's personality
- Use lots of photos
- Encourage sense of belonging

TEMPLATES

Before even starting to produce a magazine or newsletter the designer has to spend many hours setting up templates for the title. If templates are not used, you will be re-inventing the wheel every issue. Think of a template as a jelly mould; it is an intricate electronic grid containing all the typographical and layout information for each page. When the 'mould' has been set up all the designer has to do, in effect, is to pour in the jelly/text and apply the styles. There must be a strict method to the setting up, though. Here is the way I work in QuarkXPress:

• Preferences

These tell the computer how you want to work, in millimetres, points, etc. Use the greeking facility to speed up your work flow. In 'Typographical', set up the baseline grid to your depth measure. Remember, the 'Baseline start...' means the measure from the trim to the first baseline, not the top of the text box or top margin. Then set the 'Increments' in the leading size of the body copy and set 'Snap-to' on all text, except styles with leading that doesn't fit that of the grid such as heads, etc.
The Baseline is an invisible non-printing grid that all elements on the page will snap to, especially text. The grid can be viewed for checking alignments of such items as picture boxes.

• Master Pages and Grids

This is in effect the blue grid we used to use in traditional paste-ups. It should contain all repeatable elements that appear on every page, margins, columns, folios, rules, and so on. Do not use a text box and then specify columns inside – it is far too inaccurate. Either specify columns in the page dialogue box or pull across rules and snap-to and create keyed in measure boxes to set grids exactly. Reposition the zero mark continually. The computer is far more accurate when you key in dimensions.

• Hyphenation & Justification

This neglected area of XPress is vital to creating attractive typography and is the reason why most designers, who hate DTP, say how lousy the setting is. No wonder, if you haven't adjusted the H&Js. It isn't even turned on when you open the document! Spend a lot time setting up your H&Js; a rule of thumb is to make spacing tighter all round to get a professional feel. I've covered this more fully in the first chapter.

• Style Sheet

Say you have to create some text repeatedly in Times, 9/10, justified, 3mm indent, 85% compression, tracking -3 and in red. This would normally take 8 actions. If a style sheet is used, however, it takes just one keystroke or click in a palette. It also labels the paragraph as a certain style and any changes to it will run through all other similar paragraphs in the document. This is when you apply your prepared H&Js. You can also import styles from template to template by using the 'Append' command. <u>Note</u>: 'Styles' are paragraph driven, which is to say they can only be applied to paragraphs, not words or lines.

• Colour Palette

All colours should be mixed before application in the 'Edit...'– 'Colour...' mode, then applied at 100%. If you have mixed a colour, do not use tints of tints. In the Modify and Style menus it is possible for the unwary to do this. These tints are for process colours (CMYK), not shades that you have created.

You now have a template. Go to 'Save as...' , name the document then click on the 'Template' button and 'Save'. To be doubly sure, lock the template as well in the 'Finder'. You have spent a lot of time creating the template – you don't want to accidentally throw it away!

Template building is a real art and takes a lot of experience and time. The proper solution for a beginner is to be properly trained by a seasoned magazine designer, who knows about such things. The basic rule with regard to page design is to keep the type sizes to a minimum, say to Body, Subheads 1 and 2 and Headline, plus a White Out Of Black (WOB) style. Lastly, make sure the body copy snaps to the baseline grid, because nothing looks worse than columns of text not lining up across a page.

Newsletters are really the same as house journals, except they do not have to be part of a professional set-up. Such things as sports clubs or special interest groups use the newsletter format. It is usually more informal than the house journal. Remember the name of the game is NEWS, so keep it 'newsy' in its approach. If photographs are either unavailable or inapplicable then use the other techniques we looked at earlier such as quotes, tinted boxes and rules. If you have long articles as well, treat them in a different way, maybe by a change of type or column width.

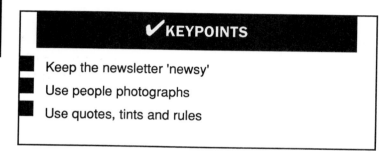

✔**KEYPOINTS**

Keep the newsletter 'newsy'

Use people photographs

Use quotes, tints and rules

If you have, as on the left, a newsletter with a long editorial to open, then use a simple block approach. If you can use a picture of the person it concerns to make it obvious to the reader. Next to it is a 'newsy' type page with lots of clips of news plus pictures. Use a tint box for different material.

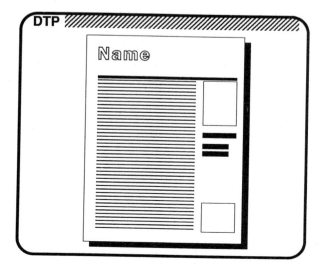

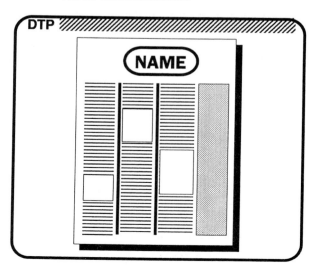

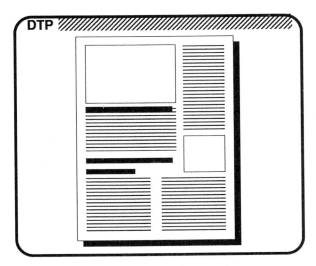

The main criterion of change is the use of column width on the above page, using a mixture of three and four columns means that the page looks busy and interesting.

Again text has been broken up into various columns and pictures dropped around to break it up. Use a strong headline when you can as in this spread.

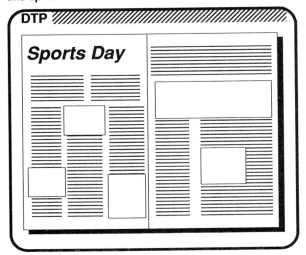

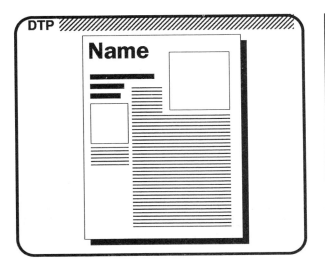

A clean page with lots of white space, using the name of the newsletter very large. Space for two pictures is easy, especially where one runs into the body copy.

This could be a dull page as we have no pictures to liven it up so use crossheads and tint boxes. A hanging rule helps to unify the page and gives the sense of hanging columns of type from them like a washing line.

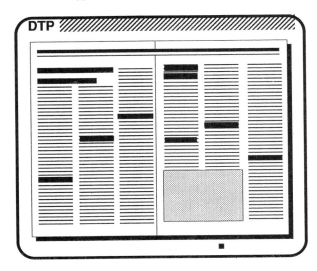

Magazines are simple to design and make-up on DTP systems. It's what DTP was designed for — the electronic production of the written word and graphic image together on a page. Readers browse in the following way:

- **Cover.** This is the packaging of a magazine, it must make the browser want to pick it up. This is done by selection of cover picture and clever cropping. Tasters, or list of main stories in this issue, should stand out, but make sure they are not covered up on the bookstand by other magazines overlapping them on the shelves.

- **Contents.** Now the browser has picked the title up, they look at the contents to find out more details about the tasters. This is your chance to keep their interest. Each story or feature must have a tiny synopsis about itself so the reader can see if they really want to read the whole piece. A photo or image of some kind helps here.

- At this point the readers flick through the magazine in general to see if it has an attractive style and feel. Now you hit them with the overall design.

Keep these criteria in mind when developing a design for a magazine whether it is a new title or a re-launch.

You can try reversals out of black or colour for the title and tasters. This gives a startling effect on the bookstands. Choose and crop your photos with care, remember the cover is the packaging for the magazine and if the reader doesn't pick it up — you have failed!

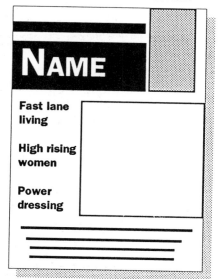

If your magazine cover is to be on the bookstands keep in mind that it may be obscured by other publications. The usual stacking method shows half to a third of the left hand side so it's best to run tasters down that side. Set a column to that width between the picture and the spine.

Here we have a large logo which can compete with the cover picture. The tasters are not in a rigid format and the picture dictates the layout. The smaller box is for a feature picture.

If you have designed a tasteful logo then feature it strongly. Try not framing the picture and let it float. Lesser tasters can be run along the bottom of the cover.

If you can, keep the design simple and clean for technical titles. This is how I would treat a non bookstand issue. Less tasters because the reader is 'sold' on the magazine anyway.

The contents page is like a shopping list or a menu, the reader browses through to get an idea of what the magazine contains, so make it attractive. Use tiny pictures of the features, a sort of mini-trailer, a teaser. Page numbers must be obvious and large. The page on the right uses lots of white, always a pleasure to look at if used wisely.

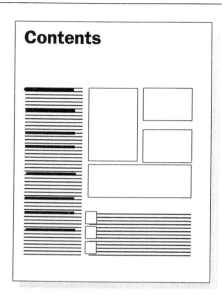

This contents page is repeating the cover picture with boxes for the ever important page numbers. The masthead is a credit box with all the staff and contributors included and must appear somewhere on the page. How big depends on the ego of the cast.

The joy of DTP is that all these content pages are so easy to manipulate. You can produce a finished idea in minutes and offer instant alterations. With practice you can design as fast as you can think.

Usually the first part of the magazine consists of a *news section*, this is the last part usually to be assembled so it is sometimes called a *flash form*. Use a different column width here, probably four columns rather than three and keep the pictures small. If using head shots avoid the continual passport portrait stuff, try cut outs and wraparounds instead.

Next come the various departments. These contain the regular articles like letters, financial reports, food and drink, what's on where, critiques and so on. These should have a unifying style about them so the reader can move to them quickly and easily. Use good illustrations to head them up otherwise they can be dull patches in a magazines. Finally, anything left has to be the meat of the issue — the features. These give you the chance to be really creative. You can use big headlines and big pictures — anything you like within the overall design constraints.

The news pages can be in thinner columns, separated by hairline rules. Set the page for 4 columns or maybe even five, and see the results — instantly.

The cover story strikes again! As a spread I have used the picture and headline very large and run the body copy in angular blocks around them rather than an actual wraparound cut out.

No photos on this spread so I have used pretend illustrations to beef up this article. By instant rearranging via DTP I can remake these pages several different ways.

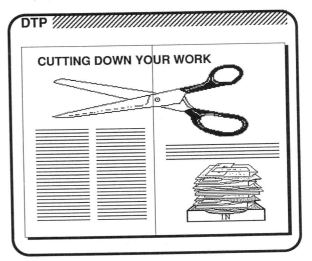

SALES BROCHURES

The sales brochure is often a combination of advertisement and catalogue, showing what's on offer and how nice it is. The usual basics apply — who and how — but now you can look at another aspect of DTP design, page shape. The sales brochure gives the designer a chance to use such things as gatefolds or non-standard page sizes. All these can be achieved on your system with a little thought and a device called tiling. This is a facility most systems have; it means you can produce an oversize document on screen and although you can't print bigger than A4, the computer will cut up your design into segments and run them out for you to put them together in a 'mosaic' or 'tiled' manner.

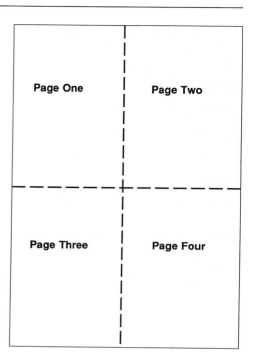

Below we have a layout for the A4 third folded brochure. This is a neat style as it fits into a standard envelope. Just set the page horizontally and use a three column grid.

Here is a way of treating a flap fold. The dotted lines indicate the folds for the spine and then the flap is cut at the thick line. Extra pages are made up for the rest of the folder and pasted up at the printing stage.

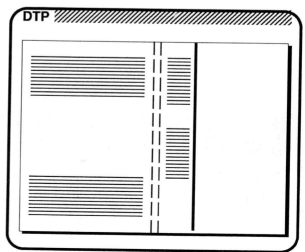

This way of working means you can produce big or awkward-shaped pages with comparative ease. The final artwork can be printed on a typesetter since these can accept 12" wide paper which is extremely long.

Sometimes it can give a new slant to a brief to work in landscape format. This is especially effective when using a fold out. All you have to do is make up your document with the foldout treated as an extra page and pasted into position at the printing stage. You will find most brochures consist of a lot of quality photographs and your copy will be in panels, or black on/white out of image, this can pose problems, unless you are scanning in the images. A simple position-only scan of the picture will allow you to place the text very accurately, then by removing the image you are left with the copy and the printer does the rest by just pasting in the picture in the appropriate position. However, I would advise you to enclose a draft laser print of the picture and text together for the printer to use as reference for positioning.

Reversals can be useful either out of black or colour. Here also is a horizontal, or landscape, approach folder.

✔ KEYPOINTS

■ Try different folds — third A4, A4 gatefold, etc

■ Consider cutouts, expensive but eyecatching

■ If material is to be enclosed, do you need a spine?

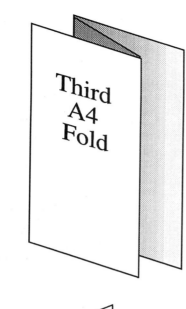

Third
A4
Fold

Left is a basic Third A4 folder, a good way of presenting information in an economic manner. Right is the other basic folder. This one allows for a lot of information to be presented as it is in effect a 6-page brochure

Three
Page
A4
Folder

A4
Folder
with
two
flaps

Two more types of folder, left has two flaps which can be gummed or open (cheaper) for holding loose material. This type of brochure can save the client a lot of money as the inserts may be updated without having to reprint the whole package. More or less material can be inserted as necessary.
Right is a basic cut out on a three fold A4. The cut out could show a picture which reveals itself when opened.

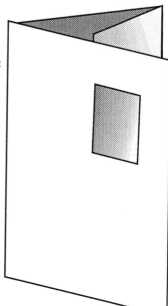

An alternative brochure style is the folder. Here you may be asked to design a folder that will hold other literature such as lists and pamphlets. You must remember that because the enclosures are standard sizes your folder must be bigger, at least 5mm all round, to comfortably hold them. If something larger is to be enclosed, like a magazine, you should allow for a spine. One final idea worth considering is the cut-out or silhouette. These are expensive, as a special cutter has to be made. But if the budget will stand it, they can be stunning, especially if the literature revealed through the the cut-out is an integral part of the design.

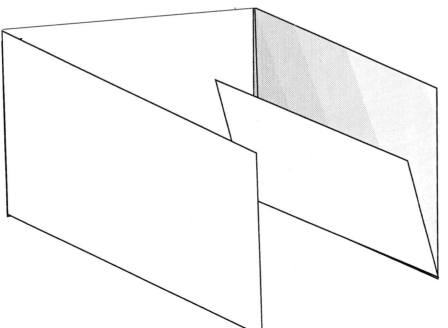

Above is a brochure with a fancy picture cut-out. The printers can make a cut-out of almost anything, look around for examples.
Left is a four page, eight sided A4 folder in a landscape format. There are lots of way of treating folders; try them out and keep in mind the more folds and flaps, the more money it will cost.

COMPANY REPORTS

Many companies will be taking on DTP just to produce their reports and this is where inexperienced staff get 'lumbered' with the difficult task of becoming designers overnight. Try to keep your pages simple and once you have developed a good style, stick to it. Although some company reports are like sales brochures the majority are simple in–house documents that the Board may require for a presentation or meeting. This means they are needed quickly and you'll have no time to do anything fancy. This does not mean you can't create an attractive document because it's rushed; that is why you have house styles and templates. Keep standard documents on file so that all you need do is key in copy and drop in graphics as and where necessary.

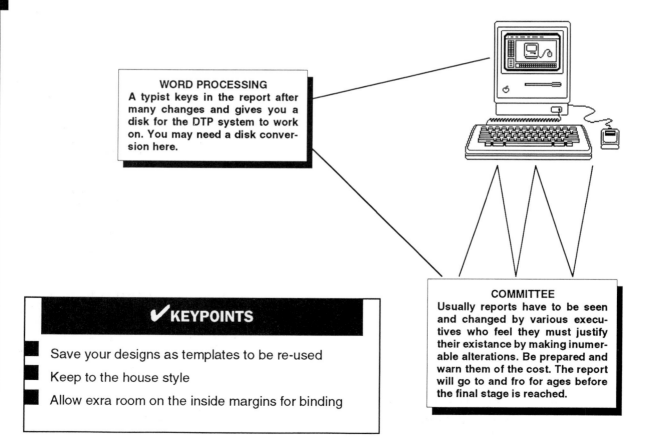

WORD PROCESSING
A typist keys in the report after many changes and gives you a disk for the DTP system to work on. You may need a disk conversion here.

COMMITTEE
Usually reports have to be seen and changed by various executives who feel they must justify their existance by making inumerable alterations. Be prepared and warn them of the cost. The report will go to and fro for ages before the final stage is reached.

✔ KEYPOINTS

Save your designs as templates to be re-used

Keep to the house style

Allow exra room on the inside margins for binding

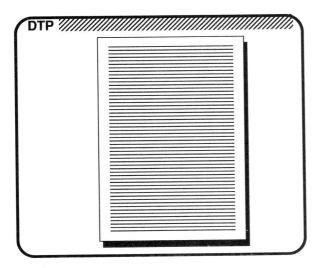

You will start off with a mass of typing of varying degrees of quality and quantity. From this you convert to your make up system and begin formatting.

Another alternative is two equal columns with a drop shadow box at the top for titles, headings etc.

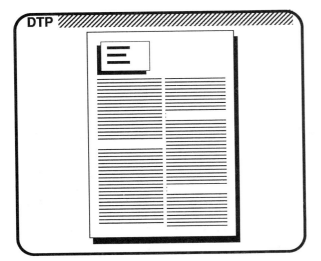

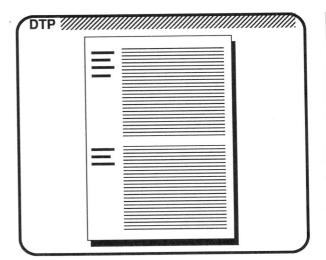

The simplest way of setting up a report is one column 5.5" (145mm) wide for the body copy and place the subheads and quotes in the wide margin. Use treble spacing between sections to give breathing space.

If the report has lots of graphs or charts use them down one side of the page and run the copy down the left. Use heavy rules at the top of the page as a device from which to hang everything.

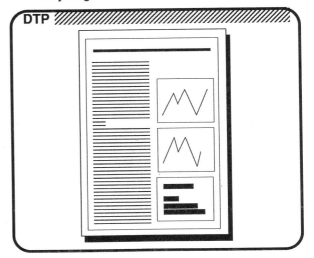

Balfore

It is worthwhile to make up, along with your other templates for the company, a standard cover printed on 250 gsm card. Have lots of these to hand and as they are only run out once they can be in colour. They make a good stiff cover for reports. Also if you cut out a panel on the cover then your first DTP page can have the title in that position showing through the cover.

One major problem is that, by their very nature, reports are constantly changed because they are compiled 'by committee'. Every department involved will add or subtract something, so be prepared for lots of re-writes. As long as you inform the client that each change is an 'authors correction' and hence costs money, it's up to them.

You will find graphics such as graphs and charts in much demand here. Again, create a basic design and keep it on file. Most reports are unbelievably dull to read, so any 'lift' you can give with your design will be appreciated both by the reader and originator. Try using columns imaginatively and use lots of white space and sub-heads.

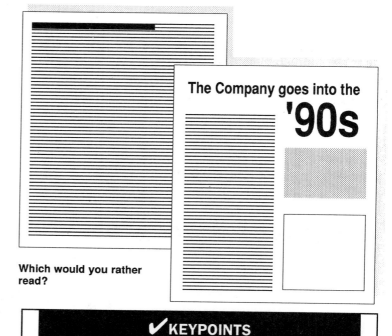

Which would you rather read?

✔ KEYPOINTS

Be prepared for lots of changes

Use graphs and charts where possible rather than columns of tabulated figures

Utilise white space and subheads

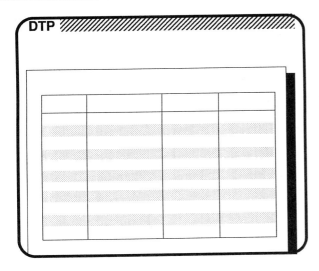

If you have a long column of figures in tabulated form try using tint strips between the lines of data as it helps the eye to stay on the line.

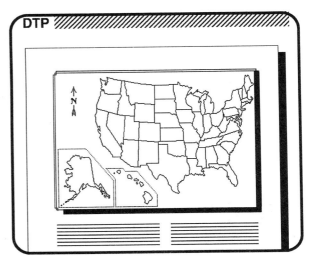

Another worthwhile investment is a map disk. These are disks which have various countries, states, etc. They save hours of drawing and can be used again and again. Save the regular maps like sales areas and delivery regions.

Graphs can be used big and bold.

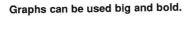

Try using rules and cross heads or titles at the top of the page, it gives a nice obvious continuity. Don't forget the ever popular dropped cap.

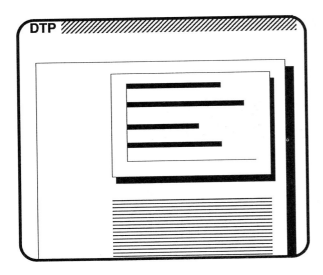

Forum

T

Often a client needs 10-15 copies of a well presented, bound and professional report for the Board.
In this example the client provided a disk with copy (subsequently changed!) already keyed in. I had the disk converted and I made up the pages in the usual manner.

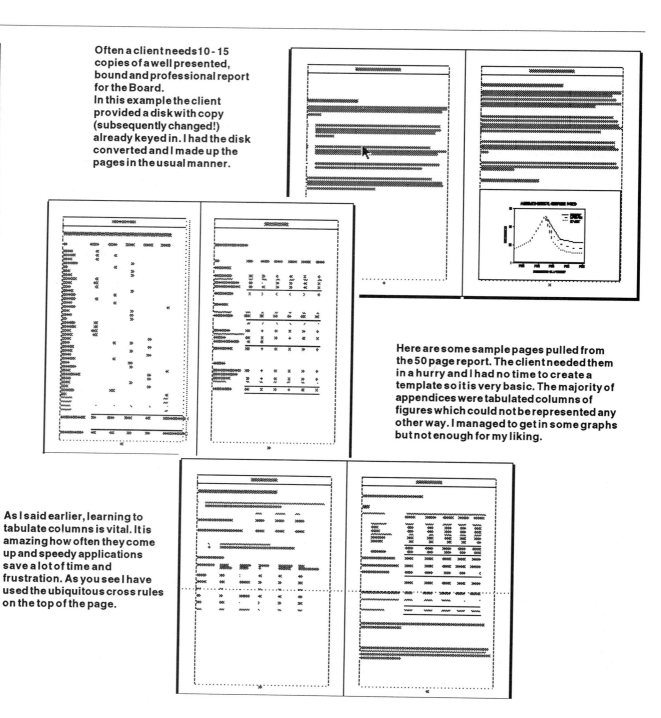

Here are some sample pages pulled from the 50 page report. The client needed them in a hurry and I had no time to create a template so it is very basic. The majority of appendices were tabulated columns of figures which could not be represented any other way. I managed to get in some graphs but not enough for my liking.

As I said earlier, learning to tabulate columns is vital. It is amazing how often they come up and speedy applications save a lot of time and frustration. As you see I have used the ubiquitous cross rules on the top of the page.

MANUALS AND SMALL BOOKS

These constitute a specialised area of the market but can be a very lucrative, if time-consuming design brief. First, create a good strong standard grid. This then makes placing pages simpler than treating each one as a separate entity. With manuals you will have to liven up the text as much as possible. You may be lucky and have lots of diagrams; if not, use the old stand-bys of quotes, rules, tints and boxes. It is a great help to the reader if you break up the manual into obvious 'chunks' of information, thereby making it easier to assimilate. Sections, large headlines and straps are desirable and tint boxes with distiled precis in them are a help.

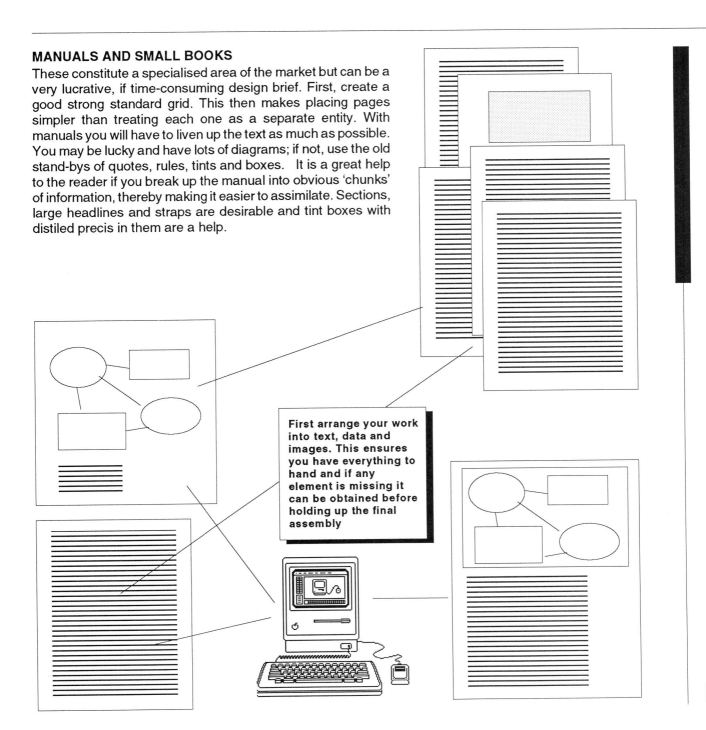

First arrange your work into text, data and images. This ensures you have everything to hand and if any element is missing it can be obtained before holding up the final assembly

Small books are simple if you plan them right and adopt a standard grid . But if the book becomes too big the file size increases and is too large to store on floppy disk. So keep books in discrete sections, saving each chapter or parts of a chapter as a separate file. A rule of thumb is 30 pages per section.

I remember in one of the first books I made up, I got carried away and found I had a section that was 98 pages long. That was manageable until I came to transferring it onto disk. It was too big a file and just sat there on my built in hard disk taking up 1.4Mb! The only way out of this - unless you have a separate hard disk - is to duplicate the file, save it under a new name, then delete all but ten pages, then save again. Open the original file, duplicate, re-name and save another ten pages and so on.

Be warned, it's quicker to plan in advance!

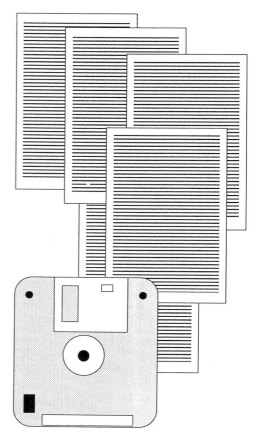

The text is either scanned in using an OCR device or keyed in the ordinary manner, put on disk and flowed into the first page. The DTP program will then be able to automatically create all the new pages required to complete the chapter.

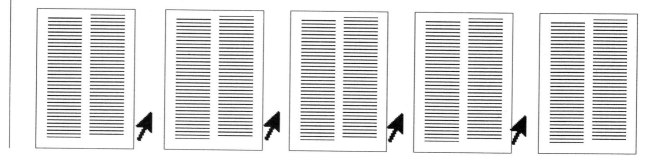

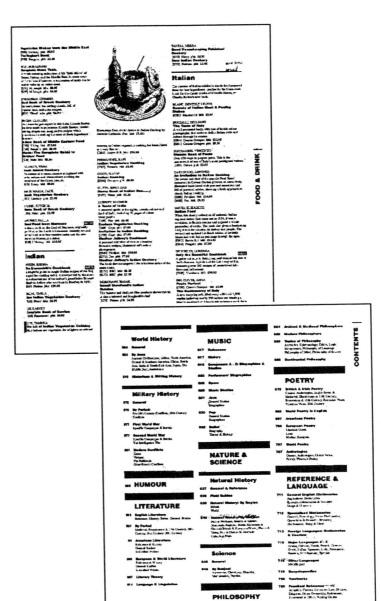

I know this is hardly a small book but it shows how powerful DTP can be in the hands of an expert. This title - a long catalogue of book titles was assembled entirely on an integrated electronic publishing system, and won an award!

When people give you a slide presentation to create you usually get something like this!

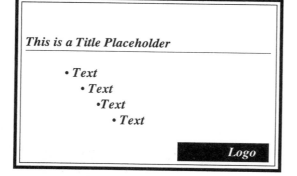

However - using one of the many presentation packages now available the process is made relatively simple.

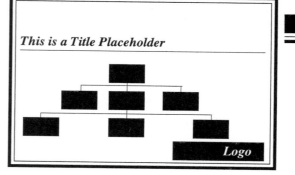

Using sets of standard styles the text is entered into the templates and even figures can be converted into attractive graphs within the same software.

PRESENTATIONS, SLIDES AND GRAPHS

DTP is a comforting solution to the last–minute presentation panic. Many times you will be asked to make up some slides in a hurry and luckily you can with the mighty system at your elbow. A few points to remember though:

- The eye can only handle a certain amount of written information on a screen, so don't try to cram dozens of points on a slide. Keep it simple, use bullets and asterisks to make the eye flick from point to point;

- The slide should only be a reiteration of the speaker's key point, not the entire script, so keep it brief;

- Don't use too many too quickly. Flicking through slides is irritating and uninformative;

- It is worth giving the audience hard copies of the slides for reading at leisure. It's simple to do and looks very professional. Some presentation software can automatically print out notes for the speaker as well as copies of the slides for the audience.

These examples of slides lose a lot in black and white but give an impression of how good the basic templates are.

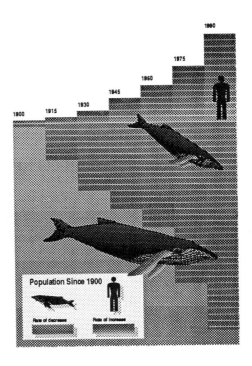

✔ KEYPOINTS

Keep the slide simple, not too many facts

Slides should contain the essence of the speech, not the whole speech!

Keep the speed of slide change at a steady pace - not too fast.

If you are producing art work for a photolab to produce as colour 35mm slides or making colour separations or sending a computer file to a bureau to run out directly as 35mm slides, decide early on if they are to be landscape or portrait. It is confusing to watch slides that jump from one to the other. If you are making overhead projection slides these are usually portrait, whereas 35mm are usually landscape. OHP slides can be run-out on laser printers directly (providing you use heat resistant acetate) thereby saving a lot of production money. If you want colour, use a peel-off colour film or tapes on the acetate for some excellent effects. Blanks for these slides are easily obtained, as are the card mounts.

GRAPHS

Graphs form an important part of any presentation so, as said earlier, you should invest in a good graph and chart generating program.

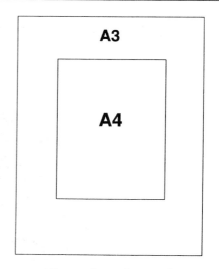

If you must have colour print-outs from a thermal printer, then use A3 size. The edges cockle as usual from the heat but can be trimmed off after without hurting the central A4 image.

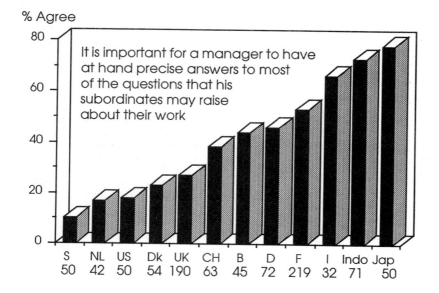

This is a basic bar chart with the addition of 3D to add life to the slide.

% Agree

It is important for a manager to have at hand precise answers to most of the questions that his subordinates may raise about their work

	S	NL	US	Dk	UK	CH	B	D	F	I	Indo	Jap
	50	42	50	54	190	63	45	72	219	32	71	50

BREAKDOWN OF ENTRY - BY DISCIPLINE

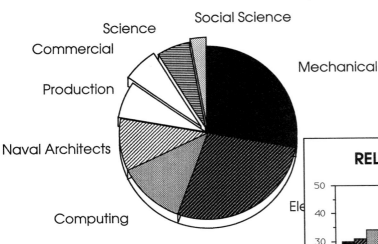

Social Science

Science

Commercial

Production

Naval Architects

Computing

Mechanical

El...

Unbearably dull and unfathomable figures can be made palatable - even attractive by using graphs. You must initially decide how best to display the facts, how best to get the trend across, by using the different styles available. Left is an exploded pie-chart.

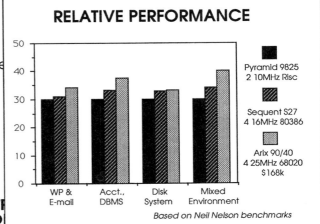

RELATIVE PERFORMANCE

Pyramid 9825
2 10MHz Risc

Sequent S27
4 16MHz 80386

Arix 90/40
4 25MHz 68020
$168k

WP & E-mail   Acct., DBMS   Disk System   Mixed Environment

Based on Neil Nelson benchmarks

FIRST DEGREE GRADUATE OUT[...]
UK 1986 - 2000 - ALL SECTO[...]

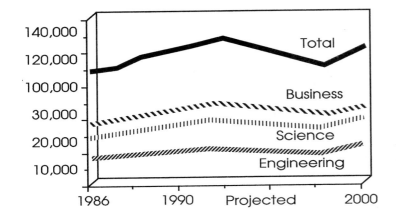

Total

Business

Science

Engineering

1986   1990   Projected   2000

Above is a simple bar chart, good for showing comparative trends in multiple fields. This one has been enhanced by exporting it to a drawing package and improving the graphics.

Left is the simple linear chart that shows lateral changes or trends in various fields.

105

Beyond the Screen

So far we have dealt with the various possibilities that DTP offers in design. This is all very exciting, but getting the design out of the machine and on to paper, or hard copy, is a vital part of the process. Since DTP first became a viable proposition, the need for accurate copies was paramount and the first clumsy attempts were made on dot matrix printers. The dot matrix printer builds up an image or letter by zipping back and forth across the plantin tapping a tiny dot where the computer instructs. All very well, but the end result is a mass of easily seen dots.

The major breakthrough began with the development of Post-Script. This is basically a computer language that describes a page design in mathematical terms. It was developed by Adobe in the USA in 1984 and was taken up by both Linotype and Apple for use in their systems. The page description language acts as an interpreter between the computer and the printer and converts the design shown on-screen into the printed copy. This, obviously, requires large amounts of memory in the printer and the computer. Because PostScript provides a mathematical outline description of the page, it does not matter about the resolution of the printer. The same page can be printed on a 300 dot per inch laser printer or on a 2,540 dot per inch typesetter. The only difference is that with a higher resolution, the image is much smoother.

There have been other page description languages but Post-Script has been adopted as the industry standard. It doesn't really matter what hardware platform you use, as long as it is PostScript. Having said that, there are some new multi-platform publishing applications, such as FrameMaker, which allow the user to swap files between various hardware stations and software packages on a network. This is invaluable for a large corporation which may have several different departments wanting to link up for publication reasons.

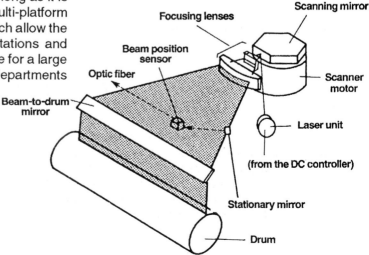

BUREAUX

Most bureaux think of clients as idiots and vice versa. Each party has good cause. I have been on both sides of the fence and can see both sides of the argument. I'll give you the problems the bureau faces and perhaps you will understand them better.

- Your files may only take you a few minutes to proof, but a bureau will take hours over a file. They have to download fonts, check the XPress Preferences, find and place encapsulated PostScript files, pictures in various formats, charts, diagrams. Remember – an EPSF can take ages to output on a imagesetter, 15 minutes per colour for example, so your flashy illustration on page 17 may take an hour to output! They have to check colour specifications, change output commands, insert film or paper. Bear this in mind when you send the document in the late afternoon, for the bureau's work is just beginning. They don't just put up a file and press a button.
- It is vital that you send a detailed marked up proof either by fax or messenger. The hard copy must contain the following:

Pictures – Clearly marked which one is which. Make sure that on the picture you note the name of the pic, Pic A, the page it goes on, p37, the publication and date of issue. Then ensure the same information goes on the output in the keyline box. Bureaux get hundreds of pics a day and sometimes it is difficult to tell which is which.

Output – Is the file to be output as spot colour, four colour or black and white? Is it to go to film? How many sets of films? If so, are they negative or positive? Is it to go to bromide? Give them advance notice as they need to plan loading of film or paper.

Title – Make sure you mark every piece of copy and material clearly with the title of the publication, the page it is referring to and date of issue.

Fonts – Don't just specify the fonts used in the page makeup package, but also notify the bureau of any fonts used in graphics applications, such as Illustrator or Freehand, as they are not specified in the makeup package.

- Spread the load. Don't wait until the last minute and send a giant batch of pages. The bureau usually has operators sitting around half the day twiddling their thumbs, waiting for your work and suddenly they are swamped. Trickle pages through, you must be able to send something earlier than 5.30pm.
- Avoid too many items that bleed off the page. This can cause the imagesetter to crash.
- If they are using a Linotronic 300 or 330 it will not print an A3 page with crop marks unless you draw your own on the edge of the page. Use the registration colour to specify crop marks.
- Remember – confusion can arise when the bureau receives
    Pages via the modem
    Hard copy via fax
    Pics and proofs by messenger
    MARK THEM UP CLEARLY.
- If you make even the minutest change to your template, send the H&J and Data file again just in case.
- If you are specifying colour make sure it is mixed in CMYK in the Edit menu under Colours and applied at 100%. Make sure you turn on the Process Separation panel in that menu. If it is a spot colour only, then specify on both hard copy and in the document separator.

Finally – if you are late, they are going to be later. If you are sick of a page, they will be sicker. In your little microcosm of a magazine, brochure or advertisement, you think you have problems, but imagine what it is like to be outputting many jobs all of which are unique and demanding in both concentration and effort. In the main, bureaux do an excellent job under difficult conditions. Get to meet them, know them, and don't be just a moaner on the end of a 'phone. Liaison is vital.

LASER PRINTERS AND TYPESETTERS

The laser printer was initially developed to take over the role of the daisy wheel printer in high quality office work. Laser printers work on the photocopier principle, using toner plus an electrostatic drum or belt. This rotates and it is the laser beam that draws the image in a series of dots upon the drum. These dots become electrostatically charged and attract toner. The toner is an extremely fine powder that works like ink, sticking to the drum and making a copy of the image to be printed. The rotating drum rolls over paper which picks up the toner image. This is then stuck to the paper firmly by heat. The drum is then cleaned ready for the next image.

The speed at which this operation is performed allows an average of eight pages per minute to be printed. However, this figure is pretty meaningless as the rate is dependent on the design on the page. If it's just text, pages are produced more quickly than if the design contains complex graphics. Bear this in mind when your client asks you to run out a few extra copies or quibbles about the charge per copy.

At the moment most laser printers are for A4 paper, but some will accept A3. Another useful facility on some printers is the envelope and label option, which is great for mailings. Laser printers can also print on heat resistant acetate which means that they can produce overhead projection slides.

The Thermal Colour Printer produces good, proofing quality run-outs using thermal wax transfer printing. This runs the paper through the printer four times in almost the same way as a litho press. Until colour laser printers come into the affordable arena, this is the best colour option.

The amount of memory installed in a printer varies according to the manufacturer. But knowing how much memory is available is important to the DTP operator as it controls the number of fonts that can be stored and the complexity of graphics it can produce. Many second generation laser printers have slot-in expansion boards available for greater memory and performance. Most printers offered with DTP systems have built in fonts, the basic being a Sans Serif and a Serif face. The user can buy additional fonts in cartridge or disk form and these can be loaded into the system quite simply. Remember that a font can take up a lot of memory, so if possible store them on an external hard disk to download when required.

Typesetters

All design briefs require the extra special finish of a bromide output. The laser printer will run out a good to excellent proof, but when better quality is needed a typesetter is used. The imagesetter, to give it the correct name, generates high quality setting from about 1,200 dpi to 2,540 dpi and runs out on photographic paper or, more usually nowadays, film. The paper is used to paste-up into artwork, while the film is ready to go directly to the printers. Imagesetters are extremely expensive and require a high degree of training in their use; therefore they will continue to be utilised by specialised setting houses only. There is a place in the market for both laser and imagesetters; the former will take the lower, inexpensive end of the market, while the latter copes with the top end. But thanks to PostScript you can print out your designs on either a laser printer or an imagesetter. So you can use your laser printer to proof pages and then send your final computer file to the bureau that has an imagesetter so that you get the high quality needed for artwork. Such typesetting bureaux are everywhere, to keep up with the explosion in DTP output. Most typesetting firms have gone over to DTP bureau work just in order to survive.

I suggest you create a checklist for when you send a document to the typesetters to ensure you haven't forgotten anything.

HAVE YOU...
- COPIED THE CORRECT DOCUMENT?
- INCLUDED ANY EPSFS, TIFFS, PICTS?
- INCLUDED A LASER PROOF?
- NOTED THE FONTS USED?
- SPECIFIED TYPE OF OUTPUT – FILM, PAPER AND RESOLUTION?
- INCLUDED PHOTOS FOR SCANNING?
- MARKED THE DISK, PICTURES AND PROOFS CLEARLY?
- GIVEN A CONTACT 'PHONE NUMBER?

Standard PC or word processor...

...produces a 5.25" disk in MS-DOS — no use to the designer, but all the text is on there.

So a disk converter makes it into a compatible 3.5" disk...

...for the designer to use in making up the document.

DISK CONVERSION

Most typesetters offer disk conversion in their bureau services. What this basically means is that they can translate a disk of one size and language into another using an expensive converter. Currently the only problem arises when a client or journalist is using the Amstrad PCW Locoscript disks which are totally unique to that particular machine. They have to be 'hotwired' to the host computer and sent via a modem-type link as the disk won't fit any normal drive. Most designers can accept a word processed disk from a client, written on another system, and, without having to re-key all the copy, the text can be converted into a compatible format for page make-up.

The other bonus about this way of working is that the client can go through all the necessary changes and corrections, in-house, and when completely satisfied can give the finished text to the designer to put together. A rare example of disk conversion would be for the client to make up a long report on a PC's 5.25" disk from their word processing package and supply it to a designer who is using a 3.5" Apple set-up. The bureau takes the disk, converts it and passes it on to the designer ready to be placed in the make-up program designated. If you want disks converted, remember to inform the bureau in what program the text is written and into what it is to be converted. However, most Apples will easily convert alien formats within seconds without having recourse to special bureau aid. Software such as Apple File Exchange and MacLink Plus are simplicity itself.

VITAL POINT

Never work with a floppy disk in the drive. Ten-to-one you are working on an original. Computer law dictates that any time you work on an original document, the computer will write a bad file name or crash, wiping the entire file. The more valuable or unique the information, the more likely this will happen. You <u>must</u> copy it on to your hard disk and then work on that version – never the original, which must be put away in a safe place.

MODEMS

Modem stands for Modulator/DeModulator and is a device that enables your DTP system to talk via a telephone line to another system, to send files to a central 'post box' or direct to your typesetting bureau.

The idea is a great one. When your page is ready to be run-out on an imagesetter you simply send the file down the line. The telephone line usually has some 'noise' on it, and the resulting print-out could be different from the original. So it is essential to fax proofs for comparison. All new modem software features a fault checking facility and if any mistakes occur during the 'send' then it will automatically run the file through again. Most modern newspapers use this system to get journalists in the field to download their stories straight into the DTP centre via portable phone links or portable computers with built-in modems.

Significant steps are being made, though, in telephone optical lines. These are user-specific, high speed telephone lines that can connect a terminal directly to, say, an imagesetter and transmit the data at a very high rate. This service is common and greatly reduces the time and cost involved in transporting material between designers and bureaux.

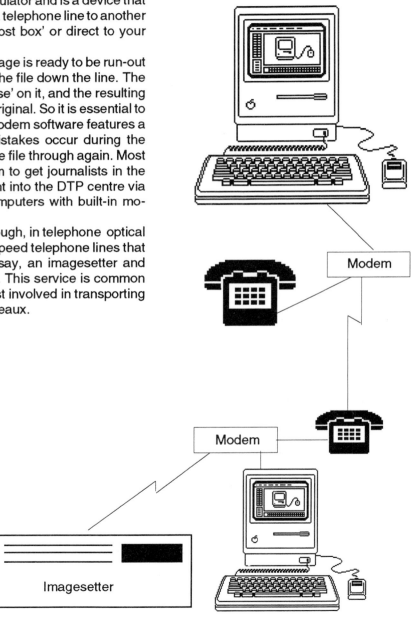

**One terminal can send data in the form of high speed code down a 'phone line through a device called a modem. This converts the computer's signal through the 'phone to another terminal's modem which converts the signal back to computer code.
Equally easily it can 'talk' to an imagesetter, giving it instructions in a compatible page description language.**

Imagesetter

Proof reading

This is an area where lots of money can be made by the designer and wasted by the client and consequently argued over when it's billing time. The problem is straightforward, lack of knowledge. The client has no idea how to mark up a proof for correction and you therefore do the wrong things and don't do the right ones. Avoid this by teaching them (and yourself) the simple reader's marks here and life will be easier. Stress to the client that although DTP makes correctiing easier. It is better, quicker and cheaper to make sure it's right in the first place. A lot of money can be saved on a job with good, accurate proof reading.

Here are the basic proof marks made in the margin or body of text, best made in a red pen.

☰	Reset in Capitals
～	Reset Bold
৩ ʎ	Alter 'this' to 'that'
ʌ	Insert (in copy)
⊔⊓	Transpose
s.c. ═	Reset in Small Capitals
l.c. Ⓛ	Lower case
⊙	Replace full stop with comma
＃	Space lines full width
Rom.	Reset in (Roman)
৩ʎ	Delete
stet	Let it stand
⸜	Insert apostrophe
⸜-	Insert hyphen
＃	Insert space
⸜"	Insert quotation marks
ital	Reset in italics
⸜	Insert word
Run on	Continue paragraph
n.p.	New paragraph
⌣	Close up
w.f.	(W)rong font

---

l.c. Ⓟ(ROOF) Reading

This is an area where lots of money can be made by the designer and wasted by the client and consequently argued over when it's billing time. The problem is straightforward, lack of knowl-

w.f edge. The (client) have no idea how to ⸜ *may*

mark up a proof for correctio(n) and you w.f

therefore do the wrong things and don't do the right ones. A⸜id this by teaching ⸜o them (and yourself) the simple readers marks here and life will be easier. Stress

bold to the *client* that although DTP makes

ꜟ correct⸜ing easier. It is better, quicker and cheaper to make sure it's right⌒ in ⌒ the first place.

⌐A lot of money can be saved on a ⸜ job with good, accurate proof reading.

PRESENTATION AND BINDING

When the design has been finally approved and the last changes have been done, what next? If it is a short run (small number of copies) then you only need to run off the required number and bind them if necessary. However, if you need a large number of copies then you will be better off sending the artwork to a printing company which can run off the total number you need. Here we enter a foreign world of strange deadlines, terrifying terminology and the prospects of expensive mistakes. To avoid difficulty, write everything down in plain terms, broken down into exact references and numbers. Any sloppiness on the markup can have horrendous results and it will all be your fault. The printer has a hard enough job translating a piece of artwork with its multiple overlays and details without having to cope with ambiguous commands scribbled in barely decipherable writing .

Mark any overlays with accurate keylines and register marks. Let the computer place these as it will do them more accurately than you can. If you are supplying laser print separations make sure they are clearly marked with either Pantone Reference numbers or percentages of the printer's four colours.

Any special instructions should be neatly written in simple terms on a clean overlay. Detail the overlays with actual colour markings. The printer is not a mind reader and could legitimately print the wrong colours. Explain in minute detail exactly what you want done and there should be no problems. Most of a printer's skill is in interpreting a designer's desires into a good finished piece of work.

Finally, it is important to present roughs and finished work to the client in as slick a way as possible. Make your work better than the standard they are used to and you won't go far wrong. This means using high quality board to mount artwork; do not use dog-eared old ticket board or no mounting at all.

Avoid this method of crop marking, the rules may be missed in the cutter and show on the page edge.

The crop marks here are cut off in the cutter. (The dotted line is invisible)

Very basic way of showing 2 mm bleed area, not recommended.

This one is another, neater way of showing bleed and crop marks. They all are removed in the cutter.

The classic gunsight registration mark shows quickly when overlays are out of register...

...like this.

Binding

If you are producing a short run document, several pages long, your client may want it bound. Here we are faced with several alternatives:

- Spiral binding. This is the type of binding which uses a round wire spine through holes punched in the margin. Strong, permanent and unlikely to wear out;
- Comb binding which uses plastic combs through the punched holes. Not robust enough for hard use as the teeth tend to pop out and messy pages result. On the plus side, however, you can open the document spine up and repaginate or insert material where you like;
- Proprietary Binders. There are several of these which use either a twin plastic strip, front and back with sealing pins through the document, or a heat sealing unit which welds the pages together. Both look good but the latter can disintegrate after a lot of use.

Regardless of the system you choose, remember to allow extra width in your initial 'page set up', as the binding process needs at least 5mm; if the copy is too close to the binding it looks unpleasant.

Finally, there are always professional binding companies which will do the work for you. The same rules apply except give them some extra copies in case of disasters.

HEALTH AND SAFETY

'Repetitive Strain Injury' (RSI) or 'Repeat Movement Injury' (RMI) is caused by repetitive movements under stress and, I feel, is self-inflicted to a great degree. There are various factors involved, such as posture, repetition, amount of force used in keying-in and even lifestyle. RSI is nothing new – it used to be known as 'tennis elbow' and 'writer's cramp', but employers and employees are far more aware of the risks involved in this injury. The symptoms are extremely painful and disabling but can be largely avoided by taking some simple precautions. Hourly exercise breaks are essential; wrist flexion and neck and back movement are simple to remember, but must be assiduously carried out.

Because the injury is exacerbated by bad posture and sometimes poor lighting, be sure to check the following.

Seating

Your chair should be adjustable up and down and backwards and forwards with good support for the the lumbar or lower part of the back. It should have five stems with wheels for stability. Is it broken? Journalists and designers are notorious for wrecking furniture because of hard usage. Replace it!
Check that it is adjusted properly, so that when you sit at your chair your feet are comfortably flat on the floor. If they are not, and the seat won't lower any more, or if there is pressure on the underside of your thighs, you should get a foot rest.

Desk

Do your legs go under the desk easily when the seat is correctly adjusted? There should be at least 27" from floor to underside. If it is too high it will cause strain. Have you got a pile of rubbish under the desk? If so, move it! There should also be plenty of room to push the screen to your correct reading distance – straight in front of you – not at an angle.

Position

The angle between your upper and lower arm should be 90° or more. The angle between your upper and lower leg should be 90° or more with your feet flat on the floor. These angles are important for protection against injury and to help achieve comfortable posture. Ensure that the screen is tilted to the correct angle. Check these angles by getting a colleague to help you. The keyboard should ideally be slightly higher than your elbows, your hands no more than 20° above horizontal. Imagine you are playing a piano. I find the new wrist rests a boon to tired wrists. These are padded bars than you place in front of the keyboard, but the best answer is to move your *hands* not your wrists. Adjust the keyboard tilt, to see which position feels the best.

Finally, when moving the mouse, make sure that you move the whole arm. Don't rest the arm on the desk and just move it with your wrist action.

Eye fatigue

If you focus on anything for a long time the eyes get very tired, especially when close up – say less than ten feet away. Although it doesn't seem to cause irreparable damage to the eyes it is annoying, so take frequent breaks and focus on things far away for a time. I think the One Hour and Break is vital.

So is having your eyes checked regularly. You may not need glasses for ordinary life, but the monitor's closeness can require some optical help.

Electromagnetic emissions

Most hardware manufacturers are aware of these low frequency emissions from computers and try to get them lower still, but they don't seem to pose a health risk that is noticeable.

Reflection

If you can see a reflection of a window, or a light or any bright surface, on your VDU screen there is something wrong and you should attend to it immediately. Windows should be fitted with blinds that are closed especially on sunny days. Don't face or back on to a window. The best lights are fitted with diffusers or baffles which prevent lights reflecting. Screen reflections cause eyestrain and visual fatigue. Also you unconsciously twist or alter your posture to avoid the glare and your posture goes wrong again. Ensure you have the screen brightness adjusted to the correct level and contrast.

Laser printers

Some laser printers emit a slight amount of ozone when printing, so it essential the area that they are located in is well ventilated.

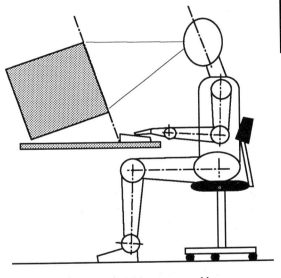

Screen angles, seat position, arm and leg angles, shown here, may give you an idea of how you should be sitting. Get a colleague to help. And check that there are no boxes or rubbish and so forth under the desk.

THE FUTURE AND ELECTRONIC PUBLISHING

As a devout convert I can see a rosy future for DTP, but only if the design world accepts that it can be as useful as typesetting or rub-down lettering. It is a wonderful tool and as such could help to meet impossible deadlines and difficult briefs. It also puts the facility for high quality artwork in the hands of the general public. Designers must stop treating DTP as a poor relative and find the infinite capacity and possibilities in the system.

The next few years will see colour lasers becoming more common through price cuts, and systems in general will become cheaper. Also, laser printer resolution may improve to the point that it will become almost indistinguishable from imagesetting. Software will also improve; whether you like it or not, the studio that is not using DTP will be a a dinosaur.

Not only the design industry but journalism and printing in general must accept that this is the way things will be done in the future, and the sooner they get used to it and fluent in its use the better. Lasers and other desktop devices produce high quality film ready for the platemakers, thereby cutting out one process altogether. Journalists will be direct keying stories and designers making up on screen as a matter of course.

Desktop repro

It is now possible to produce full colour page make-up on a desktop system that is compatible with the vastly more expensive scanning and planning set-ups at colour reproduction firms. Using software based on QuarkXPress, for example, the designer can scan in colour transparencies or photographs and incorporate them into a full colour page layout. The pages can then be proofed on a four-colour thermal printer. The final pages can then be sent with the transparencies to the printing company which will substitute high quality colour reproductions for the low quality scans used to help the design process. This isn't the future, it's already happening.

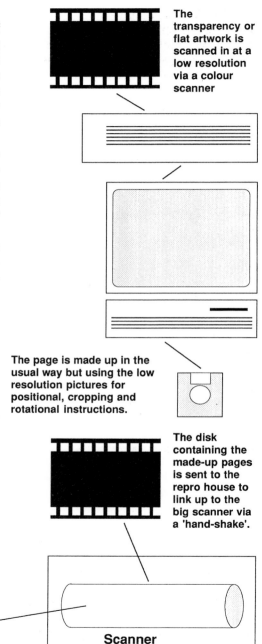

The transparency or flat artwork is scanned in at a low resolution via a colour scanner

The page is made up in the usual way but using the low resolution pictures for positional, cropping and rotational instructions.

The disk containing the made-up pages is sent to the repro house to link up to the big scanner via a 'hand-shake'.

The transparencies are re-scanned, this time at high resolution and inserted in the made-up page following the crop, rotation and sizing instructions programmed by the designer.

Scanner

Electronic publishing

Although the printed page will probably never disappear, the era of electronic publishing and multi-media is upon us. Instead of daily papers we will have a television newspaper updated as you watch the screen. Articles of interest will be called up and input facilities will be improved. Whole magazines will be shown on your ordinary TV screens. Specialist titles will be available on cable TV, CD, video or tape and found in libraries, as books are today.

This leads us into a whole new industry — multi-media or electronic publishing. Books, magazines, periodicals, and even encyclopedias will appear on screen instead of the printed page. A reader will be able to call up DIY facilities and mend his car, fix the plumbing or check a 'phone number by using his TV and 'phone link. Designers will be needed to present this, as always, in an attractive manner. Already there are huge tomes on CDs which can hold vast amounts of text and pictures and be called up in glorious colour on your screen. Encyclopedias and educational aids, using interactive screens, are a natural outcome of this burgeoning sector of the industry.

Which brings us neatly back to where we began. Multi-media must be the ultimate form of communication, immediate, attractive and extremely cheap. Beamed by satellite and run through cables or on compact disk, the written word and graphic image will still excite and entertain the world, and the designer will still play a vital, albeit changed, part.

And we might even save a few trees into the bargain.

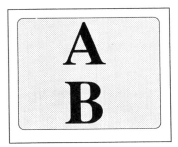

The 'electronic browser' decides on a topic and calls up more information through a telephone link.

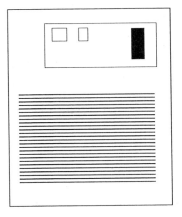

A central database holding vast amounts of information relays the specific details to the subscriber...

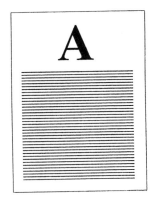

If necessary, hard copy may be run out for filing.

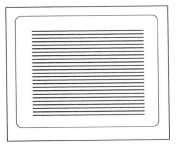

... where it is displayed on screen. Further information may then be requested via sub-headings and the whole process continues.

Glossary

Additive colours	red, green and blue that together produce white light.
Align	to make a body of type or a image butt up to a line exactly, either horizontally or vertically.
Alpha channel	an 8-bit channel kept by some applications for masking or extra colour information in image processing.
Anti-aliasing	the rendering of sharp objects to a smooth blend with the background.
Archiving	saving a document to a permanent storage device such as an optical disk.
Artwork	usually meaning camera-ready base art, it used to mean the final stage of a design job when all the separate elements had been combined, i.e. pictures, images and text.
ASCII	American Standard Code for Information Interchange (8-bit information chunks).
Ascender	the stem of a lower case letter which rises above the x-height, such as on h and k.
Back-up	essential practice of copying from hard disk on to floppy disk, work and applications, so that if system fails, all is not lost.
Banner	page title that carries across the top of a page usually in the form of a strap.
Bezier curves	a curve that is defined by points set along its arc.
Bit	binary digit, the smallest unit of information on a computer. Either on or off.
Bitmap	a pixel or dot that combined, makes up an image or letter. Each dot is a binary digit or bit (0-1) and they make up a map of the image.
Bleed	when text or graphics flow off the total page area, not just the print area.
Body type	the typeface used for the bulk of the text on a page.
Boot-up	techno-jargon for 'switching the computer on'.
Bromide	high quality photographic paper which gives the finished run-out from a typesetter, it has to be processed like a photograph as opposed to a laser print.
Buffer	storage device that stores pages for the printer, so releasing the computer to carry on working.
Bullet	one of these - •
Byte	eight bits, this is the standard unit of measuring a file.
Camera-ready	finished artwork ready for the printer to make film and plates with no modifications.
Caps	short for capital letters.
Caption	the text that give an explanation of a picture or image.
Cast-off	the old method of calculating how much space a given number of characters would require.
Cicero	a measurement for type.
Collation	final correct ordering of pages.
Colour separations	pages printed to represent single colours for a multi-coloured document.
Column	a pillar of type, literally, meaning a block of upright text.
Column rule	a thin line that separates one column from the next.
Continuous tone	a photograph.
Crash	this happens, basically, when you ask the computer to do too many things at once, it down-tools and sulks. Needn't be critical if you have saved regularly.
Cropping	trimming of a photograph or image ready for positioning on a page.
Crosshead	a minor headline in the body of text to give 'breathing space' to the reader's eye.
Cursor	flashing point on screen telling the operator the position where work can occur.
CMYK	the four process colours – cyan, magenta, yellow, black.
Descender	the opposite of ascender, the stem of a letter that drops below the x-height, such as on g and y.
Delete	to remove a word or image from the page.

Digitise	to translate an image into binary information to be stored and used in the computer.
Disk	storage media for computer files; either floppy – meaning removable – or hard – meaning built-in.
Double page spread	or DPS; two pages facing each other usually designed as a single entity.
Double paragraph	using two hard-returns to put space between a paragraph.
Downloadable fonts	typefaces kept in a computer's memory and downloaded to the laser printer's memory when specified.
DPI	dots per inch, the method of showing printing resolution of an image, e.g. 300 DPI is usual on the standard laser printer.
Driver	the program that communicates with a printer.
Drop cap	a capital letter that begins a body of copy and is larger than the type taking up extra lines below.
DTP	desktop publishing, an expression coined by Paul Brainerd, founder of the Aldus Corporation, meaning electronic page composition – the combination of text and graphics on a personal computer.
Em	a unit of measure, now widely agreed to be equal to 12 points (one sixth of an inch).
Embedded codes	invisible instructions to the computer about where text and formatting sits on a page.
En	unit half an em wide.
EPS	encapsulated PostScript files created by graphics programs, ready to export to page make-up.
Floppy disk	small magnetic storage device for computer data.
Flush right/left	type aligned with the left or right of a design.
Folio	the page number.
Font	a complete set of type of a given face, size and weight.
Footer	line of information at the bottom of a page.
Full point	full stop.
Galley proof	first run out of type set in long columns ready for sub-editing or correction.
Greeking	indication of type by using grey lines or bars. Reduces time taken in screen re-drawing.
Greyscale	an arbitrary digital representation of the amount of grey on a continuous tone.
Grid	invisible format of a page, to position type and images in a consistent pattern.
Gutters	white space between columns of type.
HLS	hue, lightness and saturation, used in colour specification.
Halftone	a photograph that has been rendered into dots ready for printing.
Hard disk	large capacity, non-removable storage device, essential to quality DTP.
Header	information set along the top of a page such as chapter title or author.
Headline	main title of an article or design.
H and J	hyphenation and justification.
Imposition	final stage of make-up by the printing company where pages are laid out, printed on both sides and when trimmed and collated will place the pages in the right order.
Image	any graphic that is not type; can be a photograph, graph or design.
Indent	to move text in from the margin.
Justify	to align text flush left and right, giving a square appearance to the block of type.

Kerning	moving characters closer together to improve readability.
Layout	combination of text and graphics on a page.
l.c.	lower case.
Leading	spacing between lines of type. Expressed as 10/12 (10 point type on 12 point leading).
Logo	instantly recognisable design unique to a company or organisation. Can be graphic or text.
Lower case	the smaller characters in a font.
Master	finished page.
Masthead	the main title of a document, such as the name of a magazine.
Menu	a selection of computer commands.
Mock-up	rough design of publication or page.
Modem	telephone link for computers enabling them to talk to each other and transfer data.
Monitor	screen part of the computer.
Mouse	the now almost universal vital interface between user and machine, this hand held device controls the position of the cursor on the screen.
Negative	reversal of an image.
Network	physical linking of several computers allowing them to share data and software and swap tasks.
Orphan	short first line of a paragraph that falls on its own at the bottom of a column of type.
Optical character recognition (OCR)	method of scanning-in text and digitising the characters to form live letters recognition (OCR) which can be edited as 'live' copy.
Optical Disk	high density disk that has enormous memory capacity. Similar to a music CD, these disks are now erasable and be re-written. Also known as WORMs (Write Once, Read Many Times).
Page make-up	the combination of text and graphics on the page, this is the ultimate strength of DTP systems.
Page proofs	run-outs from the laser printer of an assembled page, ready to be subbed.
Paste-up	archaic way of sticking graphic elements on to an artwork with glue or wax, now used to refer to the assembling of a page on-screen.
PC	personal computer. Usually refers to an IBM PC or clone.
Pica	unit of measuring type, approximately 6 picas to the inch.
PICT	a picture format widely used for transferring documents between applications.
Pixel	a bit on the monitor usually, like a full stop, it can be black white or any colour you want.
Point	unit of measuring type, 72 points to the inch.
Positive	true representation of image.
PostScript	the computer language that allows high quality printing.
Pull-down menu	a selection of computer commands accessed by a mouse.
Proof	run-out of a page for editing or approval.
RGB	red, green and blue, used in colour specification.
Ragged right/left	block of type that is not justified, i.e. aligns along one side only.
Register	in colour printing it means the correct positioning of separations.
Resolution	number of dots on the page, the more dots to the inch the finer the final print.
Reverse out	white out of black (WOB) copy or image out of coloured area.
Rule	a vertical or horizontal line.

Scaling	the enlargement or reduction of an image to fit on a design.
Scanner	a piece of hardware, connecting to the computer, which scans an image and translates it into digital information so that the computer can manipulate the image on the page.
Skewing	slanting an object or text.
Stand-off	white space between text and graphics.
Strap	a graphic strip across the width of the page, sometimes black or tone, with type within.
Sub/subbed	term meaning to sub-edit or correct for style, grammar, spelling and content.
TIFF	tag image file format is a computer file format for storing halftone images.
Tab	short for tabulation, used in aligning columns of text or figures.
Tag	programming instruction, usually embedded in WP copy to give typographical instructions.
Templates	a pre-set grid format for documents stored in memory and for adaptation by user. Includes H&Js and style sheets.
Thumbnail	tiny page printout, useful for showing a multi-page document on one page.
Tiling	method of printing oversize pages.
Tints	a screen of dots that can vary in size and density to provide a variety of shades.
Typeface	a particular variety of type, such as Times or Avant Garde.
Typesetter	a high quality printing device, such as a Linotronic or Compugraphic, outputting bromide or film at up to 2,500 dots per inch.
WIMP	stands for windows, icons, menus and pointer.
WYSIWYG	pronounced wizzywig, meaning what you see is what you get. (Almost!)
Widow	the short last line of a paragraph that has run round to the top of a column or page.
Window	a method of viewing work on a screen. Windows can provide layers of different mini-screens to show various portions of a job.
Wraparound	to wrap text automatically around regular/irregular shaped graphics.
X-height	is the height of the letter 'x', without ascenders or descenders, used to calculate the size of the rest of a font.

Index

Illustrations are indicated in italic type

advertisements 9, 74-79, *74-79*
artwork, instructions to printer 114
automatic kerning 20

binders, proprietary 115
binding 114-115
black text on tint/tone (BOT) 46, *46*
bold (embolden) 28, *28-29*
books, small 99, *99-100*
borders 45, *45*
boxes 45, *45*; broken 45, *45*
brochures, folder style 93, *92-93*
bureaux 107-108

capital letters (caps) 28, *28-29*
captions 26, *26*
casting off 17
catalogues 73, *73*
character count 17
charts *see* graphs and charts
client changeability factor 60
client presentations 114-115
colour; temperature, mood and meaning 48-49
colour defining menus 52, *52-53*
colour matching 50, *49-50*
colour monitors 55
colour proofs 50
colour separations 51, *51*
colour specifying 54; methods 55
columns 32, *32*
comb binding 115
communication 70-71; advertisements 70-72, *70-75*;
    effective 4
company reports ; committee changes 94-97, *94-97*
computer typefaces 30, *30*
contents, magazine 86
contents page, magazines *88*
copies, accurate 106
copy, amount of affecting type 17-20
covers: magazine; standard, quality printing 86, *86*
creativity, advertisements 74, *74-79*
cropping 43, *43*
crossheads 22, *22-23*
cut-out *43*

decorative devices 45, *45*
design, and effective communication 4-5
design sense 2
designer squint 21
desktop publishing *see* DTP
desktop reproduction 118
diagrams 35

dingbats 35
disk conversion 111, *111*
double overlaps 45
drawing packages 40-41, *40-41*; type manipulation 32, *32*
DTP: a design tool 2; immediacy of 6; limitations 3; in
    periodical publishing 80; replacing old methods 2-3

electronic publishing, and the future 118-119
emphasis 28, *28-29*

fault checking, modems 112
features, magazine 89, *89*
flap fold 92, *93*
flash form *77*
flat plan, all publications *80*
folders *92-93*
folios *59*
fonts: DTP system 31; in printers 110
footers (running feet) 58, *59*
forms: invoices and questionnaires; self-duplicating 67, *66*
Framemaker 106

graphs and charts 35, *41*, 42, *42*
grids 9, *8-11*, 82

halftones: problem to scanners 38; scanned in 34
head shots 88; solutions 43
headers (running heads) 58, *59*
headlines 21, 71, 76, 85; snappy 75
health and safety 116-117, *117*
house journals, market and image 81, *81*
house style 60, *60*
hyphenation and justification 14-15, *14-15*, 82

illustrations 35, *35*, *41*; magazines 89
image positioning 21
images 34, *34-35*
imagesetter 110
introductions 26
invoices 67, *66*
italic 28-29

kerning 20, *20*

landscape format, brochures 93
laser printers 109; colour 50; making OHP slides 104
laser prints 3
leading 18, *18*
letter and word spacing 15, *15*, 18, *19*
letterheads 64, *64-65*
library disks 35
light, reflected and transmitted 48, *48*

logos 35, 60, *60*; allusive 62, *63*; magazine covers *87*; type style *62-63*

magazines 86-89,*86-89*; technical *87*
manuals and small books 99, *99-100*
map disks 35
margins 8-9, *8*
master pages 82
modems 112, *122*
motifs 35

news page 89, *89*
newsletters 84, *84*
newspapers and magazines 80, *80-81*

object oriented artwork 36, *36*
optical character recognition (OCR) 39, *39, 100*
orphans 57, *57*

page description language 106
page make-up systems; with full colour 52
page numbers *59*; contents page 86
page shape 90
pamphlets, fliers and tickets 70, *70-71*
photographs 34; problem to scanners 36
postioning, in brochures 91
PostScript (page description language) 106
preferences 82
presentation and binding 114
presentation software 104
presentations, slides and graphs 104-106, *104-106*
price lists 73, *73*
printer memory 110
printers: dot matrix106, laser 105, 106, thermal, 50, 106
proof marks *113*
proof reading 113

questionnaires, design 68, *68-69*
quotes *47*

ranging type 18, *19*
reading path 27, *27*
reply coupons 78
reversals 56, *56*
RSI (repetitive strain injury) 116-117
rules 44, *44*; catalogues and price lists 73, *73*; heavy 95

sales brochures 90-91, *90-91*
sans serif face 24, *24*
scanners: handling halftones/photos difficulties 38, *38*; resolution choice 36, colour scanners 39
screen typefaces 30

serif face; and reversals 24, *24*
shadowed emphasis 28
slide presentations 102-105, *102-105*
slides: hard copies 103; landscape or portrait 104; overhead projection (OHP) 104 ; simplicity essential 103
small caps 28
software: drawing packages 40-41, *40-41*; full colour page make-up 49-52 ; future improvements 118; legal require ments 107; optical character recognition (OCR) 39; presentation 103; for special effects 32
spiral binding 115
style sheets 83
subheadings 22, *22-23*

templates 12, 82
telephone lease lines 112
text: from WP program 21; organisation of 99, 100, *100*; scanned in using OCR 100
text blocks 6, *6-7*
text flow 58, *58*
text organisation 99, *99*
text wraps and flows 32, 57, *57*
thermal wax printers 118
tickets 72, *72*
tiling 90
tint boxes 46, *46*, 84
tint strips 97
tints 46, *46*
trademarks 60, *60-61*
tweaking 60
type; weight and shade 17, *16-17*
type width 33
typefaces 24-26, 31; on DTP systems matching to job 25; screen 30; special effects 32, *32*
typesetters 110
typesetting bureaux 107-108; range of typefaces 31, 108
typesize 21, *21*
typography, shapes in 6, *6-7*

underline 28
unique selling point (USP) 74

white, as a background 52
white out of black (WOB) 56, *56*
white out of tone (WOT) 46, *46*
white space 85
widows 57, *57*
WOB box 56, *56*
word processing, for company reports 95
word processing package 21
word spacing 15, *15*

Credits

I would to thank various people and companies for their help in preparing this book.

Firstly, thanks to Aldus for the use of their PageMaker, Freehand and Persuasion software packages. The book was completely made up in PageMaker v4, with most of the effects and drawings done in Freehand, the slides were generated or copied from Persuasion.

Text was word processed in MicroSoft Word.

Thanks to Stuart Jenson and staff at FontWorks for their help and advice regarding fonts. Invaluable advice came from Mark Anderson, Roger Fuller, Pete Yeo, Fiona Pye, Dave Lipsey and Yanny.

I would like to thank Linotype for the illustration on p109 and Watersons for their catalogue examples on p101.

The whole book was created on an Apple Macintosh IIci 8/80 and set in Helvetica and Franklin Gothic. Various illustrations from clip art packages were used.

Finally, may I suggest any designers out there could do no better than join 'DiX' (Designers in XPress). This friendly user group is for anyone involved in new technology production of magazines, books, advertisements or any kind of graphics. Regular meetings and the newsdisk make it a must. Contact Claire Newton at 41 Mitchell Street, London EC1V 3QD, England.